Change Everything
by
Changing Nothing

5 Steps to Loving Your Life

and Have It Be the Way You Want

Jenny La Fontaine

Jenny La Fontaine
Jenny@ArchAngelAlignments.com
ArchAngelAlignments.com

Limits of Liability and Disclaimer of Warranty

The author and publisher shall not be liable for your misuse of this material. This book is strictly for informational and educational purposes.

Warning – Disclaimer

The purpose of this book is to educate and entertain. The author and/or publisher do not guarantee that anyone following these techniques, suggestions, tips, ideas, or strategies will become successful. The author and/or publisher shall have neither liability nor responsibility to anyone with respect to any loss or damage caused, or alleged to be caused, directly or indirectly by the information contained in this book.

ISBN-13:978-1481168342

ISBN-10:1481168347

This book is dedicated to
my dearly beloved
Aunt Madge who told me
"Nothing matters very much and
very little matters at all"
Thank you for your wisdom, love and support.

Jenny La Fontaine

FREE Audio

'Fun with Feelings' Guided Meditation

With

Jenny La Fontaine

Jenny leads you through the Fun with Feelings Guided Meditation. This simple and fun exercise could change your life! Jenny brings fun and play to those feelings that up to now may have felt overwhelming and a never-ending emotional spin cycle.

- Step by step guide to putting your feelings 'on stage'
- Transform your 'negative' feelings into FUN
- Learn how to deal with ANY uncomfortable feelings – easily, anytime
- See the root cause of ANY 'negative' feeling and know exactly how to free yourself from these lower energies.
- Change from being immersed in feelings to being the witness and have fun watching them!
- This simple exercise can free you forever from getting caught in the emotional spin cycle.

"What a great exercise/tool you gave us with the total acceptance of EVERY feeling, no matter what it looks like. Not only will this make life easier but it will also help me to accept myself in all the totality that I am. I am not just this or that, I am ALL of it. Thank you so much! "Katharina Roth

Get Your FREE instant download of

'The Fun with Feelings' Meditation Audio Here:-

www.ChangeEverythingBook.com/Audio

Jenny La Fontaine

CONTENTS

Jenny La Fontaine

ACKNOWLEDGMENTS

The biggest changes for me that ultimately resulted in this book started with reading Eckhart Tolle's book 'A New Earth'. That led into several years' intense work with The Release Technique. I have so much gratitude for Larry Crane and the other teachers of the Release Technique, most especially Rebecca, Steven, Ken and Kris. They gave me the tools and above all the support that allowed me to get a clear look at who I really am. Larry Crane's selfless work has changed more lives in deeper ways than he may ever know. I am deeply and profoundly grateful to all of them.

This would never be complete without a word about Lester Levinson who developed The Release Technique. Thank you Lester for 'coming back' to teach us what you had learnt. You changed my world and you have changed the entire world. Thank you.

To Rich I thank you for saying "If thought is creative we can make this easy!" You are absolutely right and this led me to more ease than I could have imagined!

To Deborah for coming to Sedona at the perfect time and for your clarity and commitment to the profound work that you do that changed so much for me.

To Moira for seeing the difference in me and being my messenger when I could not clearly hear it for myself. It was your guidance and support that really got me started as a Messenger myself.

To Kerry Chinn and the Oneness Awakening Course I did with him. Kerry showed me the next step in seeing the truth of myself and really welcoming all feelings rather than trying to change them. Aside from that he was also instrumental in my meeting Randy Olson and the Oneness deeksha group in Bend, Oregon who welcomed me with such warmth and are truly my spiritual family.

To Jennifer Hoffman. Even though I have never met you in person I consider you my friend and mentor. You gave me such clear guidance and support at so many crucial moments – each time allowing me to move more fully into my full potential.

To Sara, my longtime friend. I am grateful to you that, even after several decades of experiences together, you recognized the change in me and have been such a stalwart supporter ever since.

Much of my learning and growth has come out of the greatest of life's challenges. I will not mention by name those who have contributed in this particular area! You know who you are and I truly thank you for your part in my growth. My wish is that you too gained as much from your side as I did from mine! I have only gratitude for every experience. Thank you.

I am so grateful to my beautiful children who tease me about my 'Om' work and who give me so much cause for joy. I love you.

Last and perhaps the opposite of least – to my Divine Guides. You need no recognition or gratitude and yet I know you appreciate it! You have given me more than I know. I am so grateful for all that you have taught me and continue to teach me. I love your humor, your clarity, the many ways you show me what I need to see for myself and others. I thank you for teaching me your language and helping me become more and more fluent.

Jenny La Fontaine

SPIN

Do you feel stuck in an emotional spin cycle?

One of my biggest spiritual and life breakthroughs happened when I completely hit the wall. I felt doomed. The thing I thought I most wanted felt completely and utterly impossible – so much so that I KNEW it would never happen, and I was devastated. That was the day I freed myself from my ego.

Well, to be honest it didn't happen ALL on that day, but it was a pivotal point. It was the day that I realized that these were JUST feelings. They could not kill me or physically hurt me. It was the day I was able to ask myself, "What is the worst thing that could happen if this never happened?" and actually be able to face the answers to see that they too, were just feelings.

This was not about getting what I wanted, or not getting it. This was about my attachment to getting it – my

1

disapproval and resistance to NOT getting it. It was this resistance and disapproval that was 'causing' all the emotional pain. You know the feeling – as if you will die if you don't get what you *think* you want so badly, and can't possibly live without? It was in facing the worst possible scenarios that I was able to free myself from that attachment. I changed nothing. All of that came to me through acceptance and that is HOW I let go of my ego. Acceptance changed everything!

Outside in or Inside out?

Most trainings are about trying to change things from the outside – real estate and other trainings to gain wealth, relationship trainings to find the perfect mate, nutritional programs to have perfect health and body shape. While some people get great benefits from these, my personal opinion is that the ones who do get success actually make a shift in their thinking – they make a shift from the inside. The reason why most people don't benefit, however, is because it doesn't 'click', and they don't make that internal shift.

When you think of changing your outer world (car, home, job, partner, etc) what are you REALLY wanting? I will take a wild guess and say that it is happiness. You want the perfect relationship or great wealth because you think that those things will make you happier than you are right now.

However, the happiness gained from outside sources may well be temporary. Relationships don't always work out – and neither do jobs or businesses. There are many studies showing that the happiness gained from these sources does not last either. Those who win the lottery may initially be much happier but a year later they are back to where they were before they won all that money – even if they still have tons of money.

So if what you are truly desiring is happiness, then why not aim straight for that rather than temporary sources of happiness? The purpose of this book is to show you how to be completely happy by changing absolutely nothing. My intention is to show you how to be happy _without_ first having to create the perfect mate or a million dollars. We will be working from the inside out. Inside you is a permanent source of happiness that is independent of your outside world.

On the other hand, as you continue to read, you will also see that your outside world is completely dependent on your inside world. So as you connect with this inner place of peace and happiness, this will start to be reflected in your outside world. So by changing nothing, everything can change.

It is out of _inner_ happiness that your dreams of love and wealth actually CAN come true and they too can be permanent.

So let's take a look at where you might be right now…….

3

Do you feel as if you are in a constant emotional spin cycle?

Perhaps you are working hard to be spiritually enlightened. You meditate, do yoga, eat fairly healthily, try to love everyone and everything ……. But your world keeps falling apart. You get to this nice place of Peace, and everything feels great. Then, all this emotional 'junk' comes up that you probably thought you had dealt with already and here it is – again.

If you are wondering how to get out of this emotional spin cycle, this book is for you. If living in Peace and joy 24/7 is what you aspire to, but it seems tantalizingly just out of reach, then read on.

Do you feel like you have done everything, tried everything, and still these bothersome emotions keep bugging you? Maybe all you want is a simple way to just feel a little better about yourself and your life – or maybe even have a better life overall. If so, then welcome, you are in the right place.

Find a cozy corner, pull up a chair and be prepared to do something a little different, not hard, just different, and highly effective.

Are you sitting comfortably? Then we will begin.

Firstly – EVERYTHING that you have done in your search up to this moment in time has been perfect. There is nothing that you have missed, done wrong, or should have done more of or differently. You are just where you are meant to be. This is just the next step, and it is no accident that you have this book in your hands right now. Whether you got it from a book store, a friend, yard sale or found it on the street, this book is for YOU. I am writing it for YOU, and my desire is that it brings you a step closer to the life you are looking for – or maybe even all the way there.

Secondly – YES, this life can get easier, much easier. If it is what you desire, then you can have joy with no sorrow, and Peace even when there is turmoil all around you. Never give up – you are closer than you think.

"You cannot be behind on your own journey. You are right where you are supposed to be because it is YOUR journey" – Donna Kozik

If you think others can do this but you can't, think of it this way: others can and will do their own journey. They can never do your journey, just as you can never do their journey. So let go of comparing yourself to anyone else. Where you are at right now is perfect – for you.

I knew this one well. I used to see others achieving their goals, or being (seemingly) very at peace or happy. I envied them. How did they manage it? There was this underlying feeling that it was just not possible for me to 'be there'. They could, but not me. Well I did do it, and you can too.

Think of it like the generations in a family – there are always those who are older and wiser. They then teach the younger ones who, in turn, teach those who are younger than them. Children sometimes get frustrated that they can't do what older kids or adults do. As adults, we see how children learn and grow. We know they will get to where we are – or may be even further.

Of course, spiritual growth has nothing to do with age. We each come to what we need to learn at the perfect time. I took a rather long 'sabbatical' from my own path for many years. It was being faced with an extreme situation that caused me to once again look for answers. The difference was that this time I wasn't looking for a quick fix – I wanted real, long lasting answers – and I got them.

Life is not a destination, it is a journey. It is what we learn and how we apply it that counts, not how fast we get there. Everyone has different lessons to learn along the way. No two journeys are the same, so stay focused on your own journey and your own lessons. Just like children taking a test in the classroom, don't try to copy from your neighbor – their 'test' is different than yours anyway!

The answers are right where you are

This book is not about how to get from A to B. It is not about how to have better relationships, more money, and better health. What it *is* about is being happy with yourself right now, in this moment. When you know and accept where you are now, *then* you can create the life, relationships, and money that you want.

Many, many moons ago a friend, who was a prosperity coach, told it to me like this: in order to have what you truly want, you have to know exactly where you are right now. When you are honest about where you are now, then, and only then, you can create a vacuum or tension between where you are now and where you want to be – like joining the two places with a rubber band. You create a tension between the two places, then one is pulled into the other, and you find yourself where you want to be.

How about being happy with you, right now – despite whatever is going on around you? Imagine being completely happy with yourself and everything around you, at this very moment in time. Do you think that the future would look a little better? There would be no worry or concerns about the future. Everything is OK right now .... and now ...... and now. If you are of the mindset that everything is OK now, then it is easy to see that everything can always be OK. What is there to tell you any different? Ah, there is your mind, ego, thoughts and feelings that you are having right now. That is exactly what we will be looking at: showing you how to shift that mind/ego of yours from behaving like a petulant little child wanting attention, to a happy child off playing with his or her toys.

In this place of choosing to be happy with yourself, right now, even the past may look better – after all, the past is what brought you to who you are now. Imagine again being completely OK with who you are now. There are no more feelings or emotions that bother you. You feel pretty happy about yourself, and you are in a good place. You know how you got here, so you know how to be here any time you choose. Now think back to how you arrived at this moment. Think over your whole life and see that each and every moment brought you to this moment – this place of peace. Not so bad.

At this point you probably still have plenty of feelings about your past – and your future. I will show you how to address all of those later. So just for right now, put them aside. They won't let you forget that they are there, I can promise you that!

I have to have money, health and love and THEN I will be happy.

Think of a time in your life when you were happy. Did you have wealth, health and love then? Perhaps you did. However, if you look carefully, even during those happy, plentiful times there may have been moments of discontent.

Now think of a time when you were not happy. Maybe it was a time when you struggled financially, had lost the love of your life or were not healthy. Perhaps you were just unhappy for no particular reason. Think of that period of your life and see if there was a time then that you laughed, had fun, felt good and were actually happy, even for a short time. Maybe you went out with friends to see a good movie and 'lost' yourself in the story, or unexpectedly a friend showed up that you hadn't seen in ages.

There are always events in life that seem to cause times of joy and times of sadness. What if you could be happy – whatever is going on around you? What if your happiness is no longer dependent on your circumstances?

The job interview

An employer is interviewing candidates for a job. The first one comes in and says he is really unhappy, he has no money and he HAS to have this job so he can pay his bills – then he will be happy. The second candidate comes in, happy. He smiles, shakes hands and makes eye contact with the employer, who asks him if he would be unhappy if he didn't get the job. He replies that he trusts that the employer would choose the right person for the job, and that if that is not him, then this is not the job for him and a better one will show up. Who do you think is more likely to be hired?

If you are looking for your partner in love do you look for the unhappiest person so that you can make them happy? No, of course not, you want someone who is already happy. Unfortunately, many relationships founder because each one eventually *does* want their partner to 'make them' happy, instead of taking responsibility for their own happiness. When each partner is already happy, then they have more happiness to give. As long as they are looking for it outside of themselves they are prey to the happiness levels of the other person.

Take a look at your own relationship, or one from the past. Do you need to be with that person to be happy? Did you expect them to do things to 'make' you happy? Then here is the bottom line question – did you ever wish that they would change? If you said 'yes' to that, then ask yourself why you would want them to change. Perhaps the answer is so that YOU could be happier. Now how does that feel to have your happiness be dependent on someone else? Not so good.

Bottom line – life works far better when you are happy. Sustainable happiness comes from within you, and not from the outside circumstances. You cannot count on others to make you happy, but I will show you how you can count on your own source of happiness from within.

'I am my emotions and I can't change them'

People are in the habit of believing that emotions are who they are – they ARE happy, they ARE sad, they ARE angry. When you are in the midst of a fit of emotion it can certainly feel like it is all consuming and has taken control of you.

I remember very well wondering if it really was possible for people to *change* - especially me! It really seemed impossible. I tried so many things, and they all felt good, but nothing seemed to stay for very long. I would feel fabulous after a weekend training, but by the end of the week it seemed as if I had done nothing different.

Now I can tell you from personal experience that **it absolutely IS possible to change** - and it is my purpose to show others that they can too. I became very depressed after my father died and my marriage of 20 years fell apart. There I was as a single mother with 2 children - unhappy and depressed. Now, I am rarely bothered by anything. I am happy and at peace most of the time. The feelings and emotions come and I see them, but they do not bother me.

This change did NOT come from winning the lottery or finding the man of my dreams. In fact, really nothing changed. I had seen my own friends immediately look for another relationship after a breakup -and then have that end in a similar way. My view was that I needed to know why this had happened, and what I needed to change so as not to create the same thing again. It was out of that determination that I found my own source of happiness, within me. It changed my whole life. Now I am surrounded by supportive, loving people, my relationship with my children has improved dramatically, financially I have everything I need, and my life flows – with ease.

I did not DO anything to make things change. In fact, I did nothing – all I did was completely accept myself and my feelings. I didn't even try to change them. Well, initially I did, but that didn't work. Then I realized it worked better to let go of trying to change anything! There, I found peace and joy and you can too.

You are not your mind or your ego

Our emotions come from the ego/mind – and we are not that. The ego/mind is like a computer that we have programed over the years – and perhaps through lifetimes. The ego/mind is simply doing the job it was taught to do – nothing more, and nothing less. There is nothing bad about it, and nothing to be afraid of or resist. When you truly see it for what it is, YOU will once again be in full control and no longer subject to believing that the ego/mind is who you are.

If you have ever meditated, or perhaps just sat somewhere by water or on a mountain top in perfect peace, then you have already felt this. That place of quiet peace is not an emotion – it is a place of Being, it is your true Self. There are many ways to get to that place.

In my experience, the quickest way to get there and STAY there is awareness – to become aware of the true nature of the mind/ego, feelings and emotions. To gain this awareness, it is necessary to look at the mind/ego – fearlessly face it and experience it. We have lived our lives under the assumption that our feelings are real, and until we find out once and for all if that is true, then we will continue to live as we have before – in fear of feelings.

It is merely a habit to think and behave as if we are our feelings. Habits can be changed, and I will show you how.

You have already experienced this awareness

Remember a time when you felt completely overwhelmed by a feeling – maybe grief of losing a loved one, or fear of not having enough money to pay the bills. Then remember that moment of surrender – that feeling of, "Oh well, what the heck, it can't be any worse than this, I give up, surrender, I am completely at a loss to know what I should do"

What happened next? Peace. In that moment of complete surrender, the emotion subsided and you felt at peace. It is in that place of absolute acceptance of our feelings that we find peace. It is also in that place of peace that we allow the answers to come through.

Julie surrendered and got the answer she was asking for

'Julie' was at one of the lowest points in her life. She was depressed, unhappy and did not know which way to turn. Her marriage was foundering, and she had tried everything she could think of to turn things around. She had two young children and she desperately wanted to hold things together for them as well as for herself. One night, she finally realized she was completely lost. She admitted to herself that she had no clue what to do, and before she went to sleep she cried out for help. She was not in any way religious, but she didn't know what else to do, so she asked God for help. She had tried everything she knew, so now she surrendered to the unknown.

That night, Julie had a dream. It was rare for her to remember her dreams, so it was remarkable that she had awoken with a clear recollection of her dream. She had received her answer, and clear as a bell, she knew what she was to do. She never once looked back or questioned her decision.

What she dreamt and what answer she received is unimportant. The point is that it came to her when she finally let go of all her feelings. She stopped wrestling with her thoughts, vainly searching for an answer in her ego/mind. She had "let go and let God".

Julie resisted her feelings for as long as she possibly could before she finally let go. All the time she fretted and worried, she was, effectively, resisting her feelings. She did not like how she felt, so she struggled. She was so busy with all the thoughts and feelings spinning around in her head, that even if she had asked, she would not have been able to hear the answers. Meanwhile, she kept asking her mind for answers that, clearly, it did not have. If her mind had had the answer, it would have given them to her, and she would have stopped worrying.

In fact, the only reason that we feel overwhelmed, out of control or in emotional pain is because we resist the feelings. Julie did not like how she felt. The more she tried to push them away, the stronger they got. Since then, she has learned to accept her feelings. She is at peace, happy and has wonderful relationships.

In short – resistance = pain, acceptance = peace. Which would you rather have?

Later in this book I will show you the inside story on resistance and a really fun way to change it from pain to gain.

I don't want to look at the 'stuff' I would rather float above it

I have tried to float above the stuff. Trouble is – it is still down there. I was never very adept at finding a peaceful mind through meditation or anything else until I got honest with myself that the 'junk' was still down there – and allowed it up. As much as I <u>tried</u> to be happy and peaceful, it was always short lived.

Imagine sitting on a surfboard in the sea trying to be relaxed, and all the time you know there are dozens of sharks right underneath you. A little hard to concentrate on peace!

Let's take a closer look at the sharks – your emotions. They are sharks, so naturally you want to get as far away from them as you can, right? What if, just for a moment, you actually allowed yourself to look at them squarely in the face? For most people that brings up fear, so let's look at that.

Does fear help?

Think of a time when you were afraid of having no money, losing someone you love, being in physical pain or even of dying. Choose one of those situations and look at the fear. Then answer these honestly for yourself:

- Did that fear bring money to you or bring back your love or your health?
- Did the fear protect you in anyway?
- If you have enough fear, does it solve the situation?
- Does it feel good to be afraid?
- So is there any benefit to having fear?

My guess is that you answered no to most, if not all of those. Let's look at it in another way:

- Can the fear actually kill you?
- If you looked it straight in the face, will it do you any harm at all?
- If it does not help us, and it does not feel good, can it actually harm us? So is there any reason to fear, fear itself?

Take another look under the surfboard. Are they really sharks down there, or are they dolphins that you just imagined were sharks? If you don't take a close look you may never know.

Jenny La Fontaine

STEP #1
CHOICE

Keep spinning or get off the wheel – it's your choice

I understand the frustrations of feeling like you keep making choices, doing the work, and yet, you keep diving down into the 'hole'.

Firstly, all the work you have already done has been done. All the shifts you have made have been made. You have not regressed or gone backward. The feelings that are now arising are not the same ones; they are different, there were just more of them.

If you throw seeds over an area of soil and water, some will come up and thrive, but others will not do so well. Take a look a little deeper and you will see that some landed on rocks, others on poor soil and some landed on good fertile soil. It is the same with our spiritual growth. As we grow and learn, some of those new seeds land on rocks and just do not grow – but always, some will land on fertile soil.

In my early 20's I read 'Autobiography of a Yogi" by Paramhansa Yogananda. I loved it … and then I forgot it. Years later, I read it again and was profoundly moved and changed by what I read. During the intervening years, I had (unknowingly) been preparing the soil so that when I read this same work again, the soil was ready to receive it and support its growth.

Sometimes when we learn something new, we sow the seeds and it starts to grow and blossom – but then it just seems to wither away. The seed landed on soil and not on rocks, but the soil was still not fully fertile. Even though in our outer world it appears as if the seeds and plants keep dying, notice how many more are germinating each time. It may seem as if you get back to square one, but really your underlying soil is getting more and more fertile with each and every step. So keep planting seeds, keep watering and caring for them, and soon enough you will see the fruits of your labor. You are closer than you think.

Ready to look at the 'sharks'?

Let's go back to the example of sitting on the surfboard. Perhaps, as you look down, you still see your emotions as sharks – to be feared, avoided, resisted and most definitely not your friends. Or, maybe you are starting to wonder if they really are the scary things you made them out to be. Perhaps they are more like friendly dolphins than sharks.

Now you have options. You can continue to believe in the shark theory. (Maybe for you it is more than a theory – you absolutely KNOW that if you take even a quick peek at those scary monsters, you will be eaten alive for breakfast. Actually, since you have gotten this far I know you don't think that, but it was fun to write!) Or, you can decide to delve further into the mysterious world of emotions and see what is REALLY down there.

If you do decide to keep going and take a close look, and you find that there really are sharks down there … well, you can always go back to the way you used to think. That is the power of this human experience – we get to choose. So what's to lose?

The more powerful the decision the further it will take you

"If you do what you have always done, you will get what you have always gotten". Anthony Robbins

The biggest gift of the human experience is that we do have choices, but most people prefer to stay with what they know rather than change to something new. Fear of change over rules the desire for change …… until holding on to the old becomes so uncomfortable that there is very little choice but to take the leap.

I often think of the Indiana Jones movie where he is out on a ledge. In front of him there is a great chasm, and behind him there is certain death. Then he realizes that there is actually a bridge ahead – he just can't see it. When he throws sand on it he can see it, and all is well.

My experience is that whenever we take that leap of faith, there is always a bridge, even if we couldn't see it before. Think of your own life. If you look carefully, you will see times when you have felt compelled to take a leap, not knowing how it would turn out, and all has been well. I know in my life there have been times when I have been forced to take the leap, and found things much better on the other side.

After I moved to the States from England, I had several different jobs. My real 'profession' at that time was Herbal Medicine. I had done a four-year training in England, and had been in practice for several years before I moved.

My first job in America was as a bus driver at the airport, and after a few months there was an incident – unrelated to me – that ended up causing me to have to leave. My second job was in an Herb store, so it was closer to my true work. I 'moved on' from that one too, and shortly after, I found that I was making far more money in just a few hours with my Herbal Medicine business than I had been making all week at the store. Both times that I had to 'move on' I felt devastated for a while, and yet, both times I ended up in a better situation than before.

A decision is a powerful way of setting an intention.

Making a decision to change old habits and do something new is setting a clear intention for a better life. Intentions are what create our future – they are the seeds we sow. The stronger the intention, the more likely it will fall on fertile soil.

This is not really just about deciding to look at your feelings. It is a decision about your life. What are you willing to do to have your best life? I see people doing self-help courses and getting varying degrees of benefit from the same course. It is clear that the ones who are really determined to do whatever it takes to be done with their old, limited ways of being are the ones who move into their higher self and benefit the most. It is not about how many courses we do, or how long we spend practicing a certain technique. It is all about the strength of our intentions.

There is a wonderful movie called 'The Couch Trip'. By a quirk of fate, an inmate of a psychiatric unit takes over another unit as the doctor in charge. He is brilliant at the job, as he knows exactly what these 'mental' patients are experiencing. Consequently, his patients are having major breakthroughs in a single session with him. In an interview, he is asked why other psychiatrists seem to need so many sessions to achieve the same results, and he replies something like, "Something that can be done quickly can just as easily be done in a long time".

I love that line! It applies to your intentions and decisions too – do you choose to do things the long, slow way or are you determined to do whatever it takes to get the job done? Neither way is wrong – the point is that you do have a choice.

Top athletes have all set very powerful intentions. I like to watch the tennis championships, and as the game progresses it is easy to see how firm their intentions are. You can see how committed they are to winning that particular match, and a part of it is played out before the match in their level of fitness and expertise. The emotional intentions become particularly clear in a close match between top players. Frequently, it is the player with the strongest will to win and belief in themselves who comes out as the champion.

Challenges can be the best motivators

As Indiana Jones stood on the edge of that ledge, he had to make some pretty fast choices. He could have just given up of course, but this is Indiana Jones we are talking about – and he does not give up.

I have come to greatly appreciate challenges. It has taken a lot to get to that point, because I used to hate them. I thought it would be much better to have a nice, easy life. Why did life seem to be such a great struggle? One thing after another – health issues, relationships, money, it seemed never ending.

However, it is out of the challenges that have come my greatest learning. I can now see that is what I am here for – to learn and grow in awareness. It is those challenges that have given me the motivation to learn and grow.

There is a catch here. I am sure you, too, have experienced being highly motivated in times of stress and difficulty. The 'danger' is that when the worst part is over, the motivation is not so strong anymore. Do you slip back into your 'old' ways, let life carry you along, until the next challenge?

If the tennis players did that, they would certainly never be champions. If they waited until there was a tournament before they practiced, they probably wouldn't get very far. Even with a coach, the motivation still has to come from within them. The coach can help and guide them to become better players, but the coach cannot do it for them.

Finding a coach, a mentor or a program is most definitely helpful. Having life challenges can be life changing. It is hard to ignore being down to your last meal, having a life threatening illness or losing the love of your life. However, it can be easier than that!

It seems that the more powerful the challenge, the stronger the desire to change things and the deeper the intention is to change. As humans we always have a choice. Are you going to wait for a cliff-hanger challenge, or will you make a decision right now – not just to change your old habits but to not stop searching and growing until you have found, not just a slice of the cake, but the whole cake.

No one else can do it for you

'David' was always looking outside of himself for validation. He also was of the mind that if the people around him changed or did/said what he wanted them to, then he would be OK and his life would improve. At the same time, it was difficult for him to take responsibility for his outer world, so of course he felt powerless to change it.

This is a belief that many people have, but it puts them into victim mode. Their lives cannot be OK until others around them change. Now some people think that the WORLD has to change before they will be OK, so at least David had brought it a little closer to home. If you are waiting for peace on earth, the end of world hunger, the 'right' politician or party to be elected before you can be happy … you have a long wait coming.

It is a distraction to look outside of yourself for the answers – they are not there. When you acknowledge what is within YOU, then you can change your world. If your desire is to be 'right' out in the world, then look within. When you find what is truly 'right' within you, you need no outer validation; it is the truth of you. What other people think of you is no longer of any concern.

Trying to change the outer world is like trying to start the car by changing the tires or giving it a wash. The car may look better, but it still isn't moving. The keys are in YOUR hands. If you want to change your life and move from A to B, then YOU have to get in the car. YOU have to turn on the engine and YOU have to drive. You can stand around outside the car checking the oil, talking about driving it, cleaning the windscreen and polishing the mirrors – but that won't change things. Get inside, take control and drive. Make the decision. It's easier than you think.

A lesson from Mother Teresa – changing the world starts from within

Rather than looking for motivation from hardships, let's try looking at where you would like to be. So what do you truly want for yourself in your life? Not what you think you can have, or what your ego says you should want, but what your heart desires. When it comes from your heart it is the most powerful of intentions.

'Melanie' and 'Eileen' are business partners. They both have a very strong sense of philanthropy, and their greatest wish is to help others – such as starving people and abused animals, for starters. They were so busy looking at what they felt they could and should be doing out in the world, that they had little time to look within. They were putting the needs of others ahead of their own needs. This caused them to be conflicted about how to pursue their dreams, while also making money so that they did not become one of the starving people themselves.

During sessions I am led by my guides. Primarily it is Archangel Michael who leads me, but sometimes there are other Archangels and guides. They give me images and insights to convey to my clients. During this particular session (a partner session with the two of them together) they showed me Mother Teresa. She was a tiny frail-looking woman who not only changed the lives of those she worked with - mainly the poor in Calcutta, India – but she also changed and inspired the people she met, and in many ways, she changed the world. She did not try to go outside of herself to do this, however. Her power was within – it was her connection to God. She moved mountains from within.

I showed Melanie and Eileen that as long as they were trying to go 'out there' and fix the world it would simply end in frustration. The true power that each of us has is to connect within to the Source – the power of the Universe, God, the Divine - whatever your term is for it. Then, we may not be physically strong, but we are immensely powerful. The power from within – from the heart – is always in harmony with the world.

The martial arts are another great example of this. All the teaching is about being centered within you, both physically and mentally. The one who is most at peace and centered is the one who wins – not necessarily the strongest. The Karate Kid movies demonstrate this message beautifully.

There is one scene where the 'kid' has been badly hurt and can only stand on one leg. Still, he finds that place of centered peace within himself, and is able to overcome his opponent. The thing he really overcame was his ego saying he couldn't do it. When he connected to his center, he was unlimited.

Your own True Power lies within.

MY INTENTIONS:

Take a moment to write down your main intentions for your life. Close your eyes, connect within and be honest. Think big, anything is possible. This will be excellent 'material' for the next few chapters.

At the end of this book, come back again and look at your intentions. Pull up what you feel about them. When you can be truly honest with yourself, you may find that your intentions have changed.

Relationships:

Health:

Finances:

Spiritual:

Work:

Other:

Jenny La Fontaine

STEP #2
TRUTH

How to be honest about your feelings

Being completely honest with yourself is the key to lifelong happiness – and it is not so hard. Most people want to hide their feelings, even from themselves. When you are truly willing to be honest with yourself, you will wonder why you were ever afraid. It is like looking under the surfboard. It may seem as if there are sharks under there, until you really take a close look – then you will see that they are just dolphins.

I know the first time I really looked within I did not like what I saw. I was incredibly judgmental of myself, and feelings of unworthiness were off the charts. But I persisted, and by accepting all those feelings everything changed.

Why are people so afraid of their feelings? Mainly it comes down to disapproval –basic human nature for most people is that they disapprove of themselves and of their feelings, thoughts and emotions. Why is it that people are so embarrassed about how they feel? I believe it is because people think they are the only ones that feel that way. Bottom line – they feel un-worthy, unloved and disapprove of themselves.

Looking at your outer world for validation is another bad idea. So many teenagers have taken their own life because their grades weren't high enough, or because they felt unaccepted by their peers. Adults may do the same thing over a job loss or a marriage breakdown. We cannot prevent others from making their own choices, but by acknowledging your own judgment of your own self, and seeing it for what it truly is – just a feeling – you are actually changing the entire world. By letting go of judging yourself, you will find you judge others less – if at all. Imagine if everyone gave up judging! Well, it starts with you.

I was at a self-improvement type seminar one time and the teacher asked us to close our eyes. She then asked us to raise our hand if we felt like the people sitting on either side of us were more advanced, or doing better than we were. While still keeping our hands raised, she had us open our eyes and look around. Almost everyone in the room had their hand up. We ALL felt that the other people were doing better than we were.

Put another way, each person in this world is the biggest, most ardent judge of themself. You are most likely more critical of you than anyone else. Thing is that everyone does this.

What other people think of you is none of your business.

Everyone thinks that THEIR feelings and situations are unique. No one else could be this judgmental/afraid/angry, or have made such a mess of their lives. Well, I certainly did. After all, NO ONE else judged themselves as much as I did. I was an EXPERT at disapproving of myself. If anyone told me I had done something wrong – I knew they were right! My former husband used to say that he didn't need to beat me up – I was already doing such a great job of it myself!

Look around you. You tell your friends things because you know they can relate. They understand because they have the same feelings too. They may not be having a hard time in their relationship or be unable to pay the rent, but they CAN empathize with your feelings of fear, anger, grief or whatever – because everyone has these same feelings.

If you think you are the worst person in the world – look around. There is always someone better off than you, and always someone worse off. Do you really think that no one else has ever made mistakes, run out of money, been sick or messed up their marriage? Whatever you think you have done, someone else has too – probably worse than you.

When my children would say that everyone at school was smarter than them I would tell them – "There will always be people who know more than you, and there will always be those who know less."

As long as there are people in this world, there will be people who judge more, cry more, are angrier, unhappier, poorer, richer, better looking ….. than you. So for just a minute, stop worrying about comparing yourself to them. What other people think of you is absolutely none of your business!

Susan confronts her greatest fear

My client – 'Susan', had a huge breakthrough in our last session. She kept gravitating back to an 'old' relationship, even though she knew that it was time to move on. Whenever I would suggest that she take time for herself to look within and face her feelings, she would find a reason not to do it. She finally saw that she was afraid of her own feelings. She kept the TV on or had people around her so she would not be alone – with herself.

She was afraid to really look at herself and be honest about what she felt. Her ultimate fear was that her thoughts would be so bad that she would actually die. So I told her to go ahead and give herself permission to die right there and then while we were on the phone. At first she thought I was joking, but I finally got her to tell herself it was OK to die – right now.

Since we were on the phone and I couldn't see her, I asked her to let me know if she did actually die. Of course she laughed, and saw that she had been afraid of a paper dragon. Her fear (just a feeling!) was that she would die – and she had believed it could actually happen. When she fully faced it, she saw that of course her feelings could not cause her to die.

Since then she has been able to be still and look within herself with ease, and actually enjoys alone time. She faced her worst fear and found it to be an empty threat.

The Universal Mind

We all actually share the one mind – the Universal Mind. You know that your friends have similar hopes and fears. The details may be different, but underlying everything it is all the same. Everyone wants food, shelter, love, companionship. Bottom line – we all want to be happy.

When you GET that your thoughts really are similar to everyone else's, it becomes easier to accept them. After all, everyone else has similar thoughts and feelings, so there is no longer a reason to hide your own.

It is as if we are all pulling our thoughts and feelings out of the same hat – the Universal Mind. Telepathy is an example of this. Many identical twins, for example, can 'read' each other's thoughts even when they are far apart. They are more closely in touch with the fact that they have the same mind. Some couples find that they, too, know what the other is thinking.

Take a moment now to imagine that everyone can read thoughts. You can read every one else's thoughts and they can read yours. Before you freak out about other people being able to see all YOUR thoughts, take a look at theirs! Even without actually being able to see inside their heads you already know that they have the same, or at least similar, thoughts.

So if we all basically have the same thoughts, is it really such a big deal to be honest with yourself about your own thoughts? I am not even asking you to share those thoughts with anyone else – just yourself. So is that such a big deal? If you are worried about God knowing what you are thinking (most people have that come up at some time or another – that Universal Mind again!), I have news for you. God already knows, and God does not judge you for any of those thoughts. Judgment is a very special trait that we humans came up with – clever us!!

If you have any more reasons not to be honest with yourself, make a note of them. They are also feelings, just like any other feelings. In the next chapter I will show you how to deal with them – all of them.

What is it that keeps you up at night?

There is a reason that you are reading this book. You, along with most other people in the world, have some issues that bother you. Maybe not right at this moment, but even if you are happy right now, you KNOW you will face more 'stuff' at some point. So what is your 'stuff?'

Have you ever noticed that you get to a place where you are doing SO well, you have just had a major breakthrough and BAM, another wave of 'stuff' hits you and those darn feelings are there again – in force and you feel yucky again? What I am going to show you is why that happens, and how to be OK with that – so hang in there! And guess what – it happens to everyone! It's that Universal Mind again.

What is it that keeps you awake at night? Are you worrying about your children, grieving over a lost love, afraid of being alone, terrified of running out of money? Perhaps you have health issues, pain, no money for treatment or secretly afraid that you might actually die.

Be honest with yourself – no one else is listening! It is just you and your thoughts. Even if there was someone else listening - what they think of you is none of your business! So forget about what anyone else may think. Being honest with yourself is the KEY to getting to a place of accepting your feelings and, therefore, yourself. We will go more deeply into this in a later chapter.

The Good, the Bad and the Ugly

Now that you are ready to take a look at some feelings, look them straight in the eye instead of pushing them away or trying to ignore them. You know that your thoughts are really not much different to anyone else's. So let's start with something easy.

Look around you. Pick an object – maybe a picture, ornament or a plant. What do you think of it? Be completely honest. Start with what you like about it. One thing. Then what else do you like about it? Nothing else to do – just be honest.

Now, what do you NOT like about it? Be honest. Dig up something bad about your object. Maybe there is someone in the photograph that you don't like. Perhaps you have issues with the person that gave you the ornament, or you don't like the color or the shape. Find the kind of thought that makes you look around to make sure no one is listening! Don't move on until you have come up with that 'bad' thought. (Just a little bit bad is fine too.)

But I have to think positive thoughts

Just to clarify – in the past you may have been taught to avoid negative thinking, as we might create what we are thinking about. It is certainly true that Thought is Creative. (By the way, if you happen to think this is not true – that you do not create your reality through your thoughts - then you are right. That is true for you, so just skip this paragraph). What it does not address is all the subconscious thoughts that are still there – being creative. It is certainly a good idea to think positively. What I am addressing here are those thoughts that disagree. So, for example, if you think positively about money you may think to yourself "I now have a million dollars". The next thoughts may be "Of course you don't have a million dollars and you never will. You don't deserve it anyway". As long as those thoughts exist, you will not have a million dollars.

In this process, I will show you how to actually go looking for those niggly little 'after thoughts'. I will also show you how, when we give them some air time of their own, they actually go away. Pushing those thoughts away just creates disapproval and resistance, and you already know that what you resist persists. In fact, when you push against something it tends to push back – harder.

The hall of mirrors

I used to live in a house in Phoenix where the closets in the master bedroom faced each other on either side of the hallway to the bathroom. The closet doors were mirrors. So I could stand between the mirrors and see endless images of me as the mirror image was bounced from one mirror, back to the other one ad infinitum. This is a great analogy for how my judgments used to be. I judged myself – but I knew that that was 'wrong' so I judged myself for judging myself .... Back and forth between the mirrors, ad infinitum! To Infinity and Beyond! SO exhausting!

Truth is, if you can think of something 'bad' then the thought was already there. You are not creating a new negative thought – it was already there – admit it. At the very least, when you are honest about it, you can bring it into the light and change it. You can do something different, and put a stop to those endless images bouncing back and forth between the judgment mirrors.

Look behind the thought

So now, you have in mind a 'bad' thought about this simple inanimate object. What makes it a 'bad' thought rather than just a thought, just a simple word? So perhaps you thought the color was wrong. What is the problem with that? It is just a thought, just a feeling. If it had stopped there, it wouldn't be a problem, but generally it doesn't. Now you judge yourself for criticizing the ornament that perhaps your child made in second grade. That opens up a whole can of worms – I'm a bad parent, I should love my child more, if I had loved her more she would be ….. You get the idea.

Most likely, you stop the thought process at 'I don't like the color". You do not want to see all the 'ugly' thoughts that may be behind that. You are not willing to see the Truth of yourself. ALL of this stems from disapproval. As long as you disapprove or resist your feelings, you will never get to the core. The feelings will always seem like sharks. What's more, the feelings will still be there. What you resist, persists. As long as you resist those thoughts and feelings, they will not budge and they are stuck.

Notice that behind that thought is a judgment that the thought is somehow 'bad'. It is that disapproval that stops you from being completely honest with yourself. You don't like the disapproval, so it is safer to just not go there – and not think 'bad' thoughts.

Then, do you see that you are back in the hall of mirrors? You have a thought, you don't like the thought (disapproval) so you try to ignore it or push it away (resistance). So it is not the originating thought that is the issue, it is the disapproval, judgment, resistance or whatever other word you choose to use.

One of my clients said to me "It's not that I disapprove of those feelings, I'm just disappointed that they are there again" Same thing – she disapproved of them and wanted them gone, but she was disappointed that they were there.

Bottom line -if you want the feelings to go away or somehow change, you are disapproving of them.

Now there are two ways of dealing with this. One way is to start at the top – ask yourself what you think of the ornament – "I don't like the color" acknowledge that, accept it and let it go. Then ask what else you think about the ornament – "Well, the shape is kind of quirky" – so then you let that go.

There are tons and tons of thoughts out there, and NONE of them would be an issue if there was no resistance. They would just come up and float on by – no judgment, no resistance. The stronger the judgment, the more powerful the feelings seem to be. The really uncomfortable feelings are the ones you disapprove of the most – they are the ones you hate. You want them gone more than any others. So they stay and build up and feel worse and worse and worse. You know the ones – they are the ones that keep you awake at night.

You can start at the top and deal with each of those millions of thoughts that are causing all the issues. It is like trying to chop a tree down by starting at the top. You take the first 12 inches off the top of the tree and feel so good about it. It is an achievement and each 12 inches is another achievement. You feel lighter each time. You even get down to the base of the trunk – but the roots are still there. You have not yet dealt with the source of the issue, the roots, the judgment and resistance.

So, no more messing around, let's go straight to the roots and deal with that resistance. It is the resistance – the root of the problem, which has been feeding the issue all this time. It is these same roots though that feed ALL the issues. Take out the roots and all the branches – all the issues, fall down.

Once you see how easy it is to face the resistance, you need never resist again – and you need never fear ANY feelings ever again.

In the next chapter, I am going to show you how much fun you can have with resistance! So put the 'ugly' stuff aside for the moment and let's go play with disapproval.

Jenny La Fontaine

STEP #3
PLAY

How to shift from struggle and resistance to FUN!

Ever think that dealing with resistance was hard work, difficult, impossible, no fun? Not in my book!

What you resist persists

It is sad but true. When you resist and disapprove of your feelings – they stay around, and even 'feel' worse.

You want to think about the issue (bad relationship, lack of money, body issue etc) because you want to resolve it. Right along with that thought come the emotions – fear, anger, jealousy, judgment and THAT does not feel good. You want to push that away.

You don't like the feelings, and you don't want to think about them ... so what happens? You DO think about them! If I say to you "Don't think about pink elephants", what immediately comes to your mind? Pink elephants. Your thoughts keep you up at night because you just can't stop thinking about the big issue.

You try telling yourself NOT to think about the money, betrayal, weight, body pain and it just will NOT go away! In fact it gets worse!

Just notice, though, what it is that is keeping it all in place. It is because you don't like the situation and the feelings that they stick around and get bigger. You are effectively feeding the roots with more and more disapproval, judgment and resistance. Then the branches – the issue – appear to get bigger and bigger.

Life is like a washing machine

Forrest Gump says "Life is like a box of chocolates". Well, I think it is more like a washing machine. At birth you are thrown into the wash. Your tub fills up with thoughts and feelings. You are awash (excuse the pun!) with emotions. You get washed and rinsed as you search for answers ... and find a few. Then you feel free and happy as all the 'dirt' is wrung out in the spin cycle. There you are – clean and (almost) dry. BUT - the door doesn't open and another wash cycle starts all over again!

Will it never end? Oh no, not again. Now if that isn't disapproving and resisting I don't know what is!

Most likely you are reading this book because you really want to get OUT of that washing machine.

What I am going to suggest next is completely different to anything you have ever done before. What have you got to lose, after all? You have been in this spin cycle of emotion for long enough. It is time to re-program the machine.

Remember the hall of mirrors in the last chapter? You judge yourself for judging, and then judge that too. The trick is to be honest about that. See that you HATE those feelings. You know you hate them, so admit it. In fact, hate them even more. We are going for the roots here – the source of ALL your emotional pain – and it is all just a game, so relax and enjoy the show!

"Jenny, working with you has been life changing. I have been able to let go of things that are not in my control.....(ED- she only thought they were not in her control!) *I am genuinely happy most of the time. I am living in the present more and generally just enjoying life. Thank you."* **Kathy Miron**

The Stage Game

Now let's make this really fun!

Imagine you are up on stage. There is no audience. It is just you and the stage, and you get to strut your stuff. The lights are on and this is your chance to shine. This is a one person show – it is your show and you get to indulge those judgments. No one else is here. It is just you and your own imagination so let it rip!

Now is your opportunity to BE the judgment. The key is to make it as BIG as you possibly can. Remember you are an actor, a star. You are the very best actor for this part because you know it SO well! You have been doing this all your life covertly – now you get to make it a Broadway show – just for you.

So start judging yourself. Here are some ideas to get you started!

"I hate when I do …., say ….., think ….."

"Will I never EVER, get out of this … washing machine"

"Everyone else can. Why can't I …"

"I hate those feelings, I don't want them, I want them to just go away, disappear ….."

Get the idea? Make it all MUCH larger than life – the larger the better – and over dramatize. Imagine the lady in the 1920's movie as she sweeps the back of her hand dramatically across her forehead and faints, gracefully of course, into the arms of some handsome gentleman. What an opportunity to indulge yourself and allow this judging self to actually be the star of the show, instead of being pushed aside and disapproved of.

Perhaps you are the hero wielding your sword, slicing and dicing everything you hate. Don't worry, you can't hurt anyone or anything. These are just your own feelings having the time of their life inside your own head. This is what you have been resisting all this time, but now you are letting them out of the cage and they are finally getting their air time.

If you are still sitting there thinking – this is crazy, I'm not going to do this … then start right there. There is a chair up there on stage. You are sitting in the chair. Your arms and legs are crossed, and your face is all screwed up in a tight little ball.

"I will NOT do this. This is stupid. I will NOT make a fool of myself in this way"

Get the idea? Are you starting to see how funny this is? The bigger you can make it, the funnier it will seem.

What EVER your feelings are about this – start there. There are no wrong feelings. There is no wrong way to do this. There is no right way either – there is just YOUR way. This is ALL in the privacy of your own mind, so risk it. Do you really want to stay at the mercy of your feelings, or are you ready and willing to try something different?

You can do all of this in the privacy of your own mind. Find a quiet place where you will not be disturbed. Go for a walk in the country or lock yourself in the bathroom – whatever it takes for a few minutes of complete alone time. Then sit quietly and imagine the stage, the lights and any stage props you choose. Just make sure you get to the main act and BE the judgment or whatever YOUR feelings are.

Or, you could find a quiet, private spot and actually speak, sing, mime the part, and act all this out – just for you. Act the part, be the star of the show, over-emphasize everything. Above all – enjoy it! It really is all just a game.

Go over-the-top

The more over-the-top you can be with this 'game', the more accepting you will be of your feelings. The more you can see it all as just a game, the less judgment you have. If it still feels real to you, then you are still identifying with your feelings. When you become the actor then you can start seeing that these feelings are not you – you are just playing the part.

When you do the over-the-top version of your feelings, it changes them from just yet another time when you feel and express anger, grief, fear etc, to being able to see the funny side and come to a place of acceptance.

Up to now, your habit has been to identify with the feelings. Now you can change that habit to a different one where you become the witness of the feelings. After practicing the 'stage game' you may find that you are now in the audience, and only your ego/mind/feelings are still on stage.

Try it out. Start by playing the judging role as you 'normally' would. Regular, low key, muttering to yourself, going round and round in circles getting nowhere. You have been there a million times, so you know how to do it! Take a check and see how that feels. Most likely it feels heavy and low energy.

Now make it bigger than life – over-dramatize the whole thing, and go way over the top. Now see how it feels. Do you notice the difference? See how much lighter it feels? Even funny? Also notice that you probably feel less engaged in the feelings – less as if they are *your* feelings, and more as if you are the witness.

As you keep practicing you may find that your feelings no longer need the full 5 minutes on stage. They are happy in just one or two minutes. You have now dug out the roots, the source of your emotional discomfort. As other roots show up, you know exactly what to do – give them their five minutes on stage.

ALWAYS remember to go behind the original thought and see the disapproval – those are the roots, and that is the quickest way to peace. Playing the 'stage game' with the disapproval and resistance allows you to completely accept them to where they become a non-issue. They stay, they go, it no longer matters to you.

The more adept you become at this, the less you fear the washing machine effect – going through another spin cycle. The less you fear – and resist, the spin cycle ….. the less you feel like you are IN the spin cycle!

Remember the hall of mirrors? The outer mirrors are now starting to fade. As you become more and more accepting of the judgments and resistance, you now start to judge the judgments less! Disapproval, judgment, resistance, criticism, disappointment are no longer words or feelings to be feared and … judged, resisted, disliked ……. You get the idea!

Now it becomes easier to access deeper layers of feelings, because they are just more acceptable and funnier. The whole process is just much more fun. As you really get into this process, you may find yourself actually looking forward to 'feeling' – it almost becomes an indulgence to play with your feelings in this way.

Act, Write, Paint, Sing, Dance

If you are a writer you may prefer to write it out – just for you. It doesn't matter what you write, just start writing all the 'ugly' things you can possibly think of – all the things you don't want anyone to know about you. The main thing is to get it all OUT instead of bottled up inside. When you are done you can burn, shred or just throw out what you wrote. You don't need it any more.

Anytime I felt 'stuck' with an issue I would start to write – whatever came to my mind. I would keep writing until it was all out. By the end of it I always felt so much lighter. Often, it would even bring to mind some realization that took me to the next step. Whatever came up got me unstuck – simply by acknowledging my thoughts and feelings.

Use whatever method resonates with you. If you are an artist, then draw or paint your feelings – just make it BIG, bigger than life, exaggerate your feelings until you see the funny side. Singing is a great way to do this – whether you do it in your head or out loud – sing your way to freedom from judgment. Do the self-judgment dance until you drop!

Another way that works well is to simply 'be' with the feelings. I find this way particularly helpful with grief. Imagine the feelings as a big pool in front of you. Walk right into the center of all those feelings and just stop. Be with the feelings. Don't try to stop them or make them change, just be. When you completely stop resisting your feelings, it is as if the power just goes out of them.

When you stop pushing against something, it stops pushing back. It is the same with feelings. All of these methods are different ways to stop resisting your feelings, and ultimately to simply accept them just the way they are.

Mummy, mummy look at me NOW!

If you have ever been around small children, they are a perfect example of what is happening here. Remember a time when you have seen (or experienced) a small child (let's call her Suzie) come up to Mum or Dad while they are having a riveting conversation with another adult. Suzie wants something – to show off her dress, or go potty, get food – she just wants attention, and she wants it NOW. The more her parent ignores her, the more persistent and louder she gets. Finally, she can no longer be ignored and she gets the total attention she wants. It takes but a minute and she is satisfied. Off she goes to play again, happy and content.

Your emotions and feelings are just like little Suzie. They simply want attention! The longer you ignore them, the louder and more persistent they get. However, when you do pay attention and give them 5 minutes on stage – did you notice what happened? They get quieter and maybe even go away altogether.

The biggest fear is that if we pay attention to negative feelings they will get worse. In fact, the opposite is true. If you find it hard to get past the fear – then notice that that, too, is just a feeling. Invite it up onto the stage and give it its 5 minutes of glory – now see where the fear is.

"The exercise ...... was incredible........my evil fantasy was *fun and effective and I was surprised how quickly the energy/emotions left. In the past I was in the frame of mind that as soon as I felt (resistance), it had to go, but this way......indulging the bad feelings to the hilt goes even deeper and clears out more".* **Dan Howley**

Depression is a feeling too

Depression is also just a feeling. I know from experience that it can feel all-consuming, as if nothing can possibly ever change. After my father died and my marriage of 20 years finally ended, my whole world turned upside down and I went into a state of deep depression. It is often out of our greatest adversity that we gain the most.

It was out of this "lowest-of-the-low" states that I began a transformation that brought me to where I am today. I have nothing but gratitude for it all. Sometimes it takes being at rock bottom to find the motivation to search for answers - and not just any old answers, not a quick fix, but deep, lasting Truth.

If you are in a state of depression and reading this, then I congratulate you, because you may just be on the brink of a whole new life. Depression is a feeling, like any other feeling. All it wants is to be acknowledged, given attention and 5 minutes of fame. Try it for yourself. Fully face the feeling of depression, welcome it up, put it on stage, BE it just for a moment. See what thoughts and feelings are there – be honest. The FEELINGS cannot hurt you. They are actually coming up to leave – they are already on their way out, you just need to allow them to be, accept them just as they are, and just be the witness as they fade away to nothing.

A great way to 'play' with this feeling is to be "Eeyore – the gloomy donkey" from Winnie the Pooh. Eeyore is always very, very sad. Find a clip of Eeyore – he has a wonderfully sad voice and manner. Be the part and OVER dramatize it. Even if you go just a little bit over the top you will start to feel lighter, feel the fun in it. Try this line of Eeyore's:-

"Good morning, Pooh Bear," said Eeyore gloomily. "If it is a good morning," he said. "Which I doubt," said he.

Did that make you laugh? Now try it for yourself.

I am afraid of my anger

Many people are afraid to express their anger, as it may get out of control. Well, it is most likely already out of control, and the more you tell little Suzie (your anger) to go away, the louder and more persistent it may get. Eventually little Suzie may just blow up in a huge volcanic rage – not pretty.

The <u>feeling</u> of anger cannot hurt you – bottling it up, however, may not have a happy ending. Up to this point, you may have been trying to control the anger and stifle it. How has that been working for you so far? Probably not so well if you still have lots of anger. Putting it on the stage of your own mind is a way you can acknowledge the anger safely and easily.

Anger is also a great feeling to blame someone else for – they 'made' me angry. In the first chapter I addressed the fact that no one can 'make you' do or feel anything. That is the good news, because it means that YOU are the deciding factor when it comes to feelings – they are YOUR feelings, therefore YOU can change them. The other side of that is that no one else can cause you to have particular feelings, but neither can they change them for you.

The 'safe' way to acknowledge anger is to be alone – this is NOT a time to be around others! If you want to get physical as you acknowledge and act out the anger, then have a punching bag – a cushion or pillow works great. As you pound away on the pillow make sure you are aware of the feelings behind it and OVER dramatize it. Speak out what it is you are mad about.

By making it bigger than life you are effectively opening the barn doors and letting it gush out, instead of it coming out of a 1 inch pipe with ten tons of pressure behind it. When you open the barn doors, the pressure immediately drops, and in no time at all the anger dissipates.

Some people are less physical with their anger, but bottle it up inside. 'Beverly' is 13 and very angry. She tries so hard not to be angry and control it, but the more she bottles it up the more the pressure builds. Medication is one option, but all that will do is suppress what she is already feeling.

Anger is just a feeling, like any other feeling. The ONLY issue is the disapproval and judgment that keeps it bottled up until the valve blows. Fortunately, Beverly loves to write so I suggested to her mother that she encourages Beverly to write out all her angry feelings – just for her. No one else need see them. It does not matter what she is angry about, it is just important that she moves past her own judgment of her anger – then she can let it move through effortlessly. The writing is a way of giving vent to the anger – giving it its 5 minutes on stage.

"Thank you SO much! The stage and auditorium really worked for me…….. I was spinning in an eddy for days, trying to move through a very difficult encounter with a friend. I got on that stage on your call and "Poof"! , the story, emotion etc. disappeared! How cool!" **Molly Quarrier**

STEP #4
DIG

How to dig deep and find gold where you least expect it.

'Welcome All Feelings' – Lester Levinson

If you really got into the last 'Act' dealing with resistance, you will be ready to rock and roll with this one. Now you can see how facing your greatest fears can change sharks into dolphins. The resistance that was causing you so much pain and anguish has been transformed from pain to gain as you start to feel more in control of your emotions.

Coming to a place of acceptance of resistance and disapproval is HUGE. Stay with that step for as long as you need to until you feel like you have got it. Enjoy it. If it feels like a struggle, then go with the struggle – make THAT larger than life. Struggle until you can struggle no more. That is just a feeling too.

Each step is about being more and more honest with yourself about your feelings. The more accepting you are of the emotions, the easier it is to be honest. It is like being in a canoe on a fast moving river. A minute ago you were safely on land. Then you looked at your bank account balance, or had a row with your spouse. The an ensuing wave of emotion knocks you off dry land into the turbulent water. Fortunately, you fell in with a canoe – this is our imagination ,after all, so we can make it any way we want! You think you want to be back where you were before the incident that sent you over board. It is familiar to you, after all. So you start paddling furiously against the current. How does that feel to you? Most likely it is hard work, frustrating, you are stressed out, afraid and all the time looking back to where you came from rather than looking ahead – downstream.

Truth is that however hard you paddle, you will never get back to exactly where you were. It is always just a little further downstream, as each time you learn just a little more about yourself. You start to notice that with each step downstream, the river widens and the trees that had come right to the rivers edge begin to clear a little. The river bank is more open, and now there are flowers and birds.

Now I am going to suggest the unthinkable – stop paddling! In this analogy it may not seem so hard - so try applying that to your own life. Let go of struggling – trying to keep your head above water. This is not giving up – it is letting go and trusting. It is not about doing nothing, but rather quieting the mind enough to actually hear the real answers and taking action on those.

Turn around and look downstream. If there are a few bumps along the way, at least you will see them coming! If you actually paddle with the current (give your feelings their 5 minutes on stage) it can be even easier. Now the river widens, the current is less swift, there are beautiful meadows on either side and life is so much easier and peaceful.

Row, row, row your boat,

Gently down the stream,

Merrily, merrily, merrily, merrily,

Life is but a dream

Janice frees herself from the hall of mirrors

'Janice' was very judgmental of herself. If she even had a fleeting thought of judging someone else, she would give herself a hard time. She was well stuck in the hall of mirrors. She felt so bad about this that she did not want to admit it to anyone. It was keeping her completely stuck and miserable. Then I pointed out to her that the judgment was just a feeling.

She had been able to accept other feelings, such as fear and grief, but judgment was a huge monster in the closet. Step by gradual step, she was able to start accepting the judgment. It was like peeling an onion as each layer slowly came away. She was so happy when she could imagine herself judging and disapproving on her imaginary stage – and actually enjoy it. She felt free of an anchor that had been holding her back for her entire life.

It was a HUGE turning point for her in her life. The more accepting she became of the judgment, the less and less bothered she was – by anything. She started to notice that at times when, in the past, she would have judged herself for being less than 'perfect', she no longer did.

She also noticed that she was no longer concerned about what others thought of her. Now this was really the flip side of the same coin. The only concern she had about what others thought was really still her judgment of herself. As her inner world changed, so too did her outer world. Her relationships with her family improved dramatically. She was able to create a living from work that she loved for the first time in years. She also found herself being loved and accepted by the people around her.

What she now saw in the mirror had changed. What she used to see was the judgment reflected back and forth ad infinitum. Now all that is reflected back to her is the love and acceptance she now feels within. She had changed nothing at all. She had simply accepted what was already there. The result was that everything changed.

Time to go digging for gold!

It is hard, if not impossible, to unlock any feeling as long as you disapprove or resist it. Always check for disapproval and resistance. As you practice this you will start to be aware of your thoughts and feelings more as an observer. 'Ah, there goes a bit of sadness/anger/fear' – in the moment of acknowledging it, it is gone.

Imagine you are at the beach, jumping waves. When you face the waves you can see them coming, anticipate them and choose to jump over them, swim through them, dive under them and it is all great fun. If you become afraid and try to run away or resist the waves - that is when you get into trouble. If you turn your back on the waves, they can come up unexpectedly and send you flying, or knock you under the water where you can't breathe.

Only by fully facing the waves are YOU in control and then it can even be FUN! The waves are coming anyway – might as well enjoy them! Your feelings are there anyway – might as well fully face them. We have all tried running away – it certainly didn't work too well for me! How about you? Perhaps it's time to try something different!

The 'Ugly' Stuff ....

So now it is time to take a look at some deeper issues. Earlier we addressed the 'Good' and the 'Bad'. Now that you have turned resistance from a pain to a gain, it's time for the 'Ugly'.

By now you are probably seeing the fun in this. It really is all just a game. Remember the object you were looking at earlier? You looked at the Good and the Bad feelings about it. Now take just a minute and see if you can access some really ugly thoughts. These are the ones you don't even want to admit to yourself. Check and see if there is any disapproval there, and give it its 5 minutes on stage before you try to move on with the 'Ugly'. Most likely, when you address the disapproval you will find the 'Ugly' thoughts really aren't so bad after all. They only appear 'ugly' because of the disapproval. With that out of the way, they become a non-event.

Challenge Yourself

Now, let's have some more fun. You have had a little taste of being honest with yourself. Let's do that again with something that really matters. You know the basics of 'playing' with resistance and disapproval. When you have that down, this part is easy.

Go back to whatever the issue is that keeps you up at night. You can start with the 'Good' thoughts – but there probably aren't too many of those, right? So let's go straight to the juicy stuff. The 'Bad' thoughts – the ones that are the most uncomfortable and you really don't like.

So what do you REALLY think about your ex-partner, your boss, your body? Take a good look at the fear for your children, or not having enough money, health issues – whatever it is. Remember, no one else is here, no one else is listening and the feelings CANNOT HURT YOU.

You may initially feel some 'pain' as you start to fully face the feelings. That is just resistance and you know what to do with that. Give it the 5 minutes on stage routine – or as long as you need, until you can see the funny side of it. Resist until you can resist no more. Now how 'bad' are the 'bad' feelings? If they still feel 'bad', then pull up the disapproval and put that on stage. Go looking for any disapproving thoughts you can find.

For right now, be as honest as you can. Whatever is there is just perfect. If you know there is more underneath but are too afraid to look – that is fine too. You are being honest with yourself, which is the whole purpose of all this. If you see yourself judging what is coming up –let that be OK too. It is just another feeling.

This is another moment to give yourself time alone. Don't rush it. Allow the feelings to come up. Look for the resistance and disapproval, have fun with it and watch it as it just disappears. As you do this, you will notice that the 'bad' and 'ugly' thoughts and feelings no longer have any power. As you move through the bad feelings, you will naturally start pulling up the 'ugly' ones. They are no different – just a little more disapproval that's all.

Dig deeper ….

The more you practice this, the easier and quicker it will become. So far you have been standing in the shallows and allowing the waves to come to you. You are probably already noticing how much stronger you feel. You are no longer being battered by the waves of emotions. They are not pushing you around anymore.

Now it is time to move a little deeper and go out to meet the waves. As you continue to think about this issue that has, in the past, kept you awake at night, ask yourself – "What is the worst thing that could happen?". Just notice what comes up. Now take a step back from the thought that arose and look behind it for the disapproval, and put that up on your stage. Disapprove as much as you can until it is just funny.

Now take another look at the original thought. Does it look so bad? If it still seems like a 'bad' thing then there is just more disapproval that wants some attention. Bring it up on stage and give it its 5 minutes of fame. Keep going until the original thought simply has no more power in it – it is just a thought, not good or bad, and certainly nothing to resist or be afraid of.

Keep asking yourself – "What is the worst thing that could happen?" until nothing else is coming up. By now, you will be feeling more and more at Peace. This place of Peace is not an emotion. This is who you truly are underneath all those feelings.

Take a look at the issue that had been such a huge deal. Is it such a big deal now? Most likely it is not. If it still is, then keep going with this process until it no longer has power over you and no longer runs you. Remember that these are only feelings – they are your feelings and they have no power unless you give them power by resisting them. By facing them and any disapproval you have of them, you are taking back your own power, seeing that YOU are in the driver's seat – not the feelings.

Now ask yourself if you feel more, or less able to resolve this situation. Of course you do. Nothing, on the outside, has changed. The facts of the situation have not changed. What HAS changed is how you feel about it all. You didn't even DO anything to change it – just accepted what is. As the fear, grief, anger or whatever it was, dissolves away, you are left with a sense of Peace. It becomes easier to make decisions, good decisions, not those coming from fear or anger.

After a short while this process can become very fast. As soon as you notice the disapproval, the mere fact of acknowledging it, will cause it to dissolve. Is it worth taking some time to practice this to be able to be in charge of your emotions rather than being run by them? They are your emotions, after all.

Become the witness

I was watching the finals of a major tennis tournament, and one of my favorite players was attempting to win his first major title. I noticed the adrenalin start to pump as I got 'into' the game. I first checked for any disapproval, and there I noticed this little voice that was saying "You're supposed to be peaceful and never bothered by anything!" Of course I had to laugh at that!

Being peaceful isn't about never having feelings – feelings are a part of life, and they can be a good part. Being peaceful is about being OK with the feelings, and just being the witness rather than resisting or disapproving of them.

So then, as I watched the tennis, I moved from <u>being</u> the feelings to <u>witnessing</u> them. By simply noticing the point-by-point hopes and fears, I was able to watch the match, enjoy absolutely every point – who ever won it, and still root for my favorite. What was different was that I was enjoying the whole thing, and was not caught up in who won. I was happy either way. The game became far MORE enjoyable.

"The sessions with you really got me moving energy wise. I could feel the change and amazing things just kept manifesting with total ease. I am so much more in the quiet now and it is so peaceful. (I am even able to watch political fighting going on and NOT GET STIRRED UP!!!!!!)" **Veronica C.**

Jenny La Fontaine

STEP #5
APPLY

How to apply this to any area of your life

So now let's look at exactly how all this relates to your life, your issues and challenges. So far you have changed nothing – simply accepted your feelings. Now, if you have really gone deep with those exercises then your life may already have changed – perhaps even dramatically. Let's look closer at some specific issues and see how changing nothing can really change everything!

Take a look at the intentions you wrote down at the end of the second chapter. Look behind those intentions and that is where you will most likely find your biggest fears. Your intentions – the things you would like to have – are obviously the things that you don't have. You may have been holding in mind these intentions for some time – and yet, they have not yet shown up in your life.

Now that you can be more honest with yourself (since you no longer judge your feelings) perhaps you will find out why. As we take a look behind each of your intentions, maybe it will become clear to you what thoughts you have previously suppressed.

Without the veil of judgment clouding the issue, now you can be honest with yourself. Awareness – seeing the truth of yourself, is 90% of what it takes to release those limiting thoughts and feelings and begin to connect with your unlimited Self.

Finances

Let's say your intention is to have a million dollars. Take a look at what you think of your financial situation now. If you knew, beyond a shadow of a doubt, that you always have all the money you need when you need it to abundantly meet all your needs …. Would you need a million dollars? Most likely not. You want the million dollars so you always feel like there is a safety net – that you will always have what you need when you need it.

So if you do not feel 'safe' financially then you are holding in mind that you lack money or that someday you will run out. In other words, you want to change your current and future situation – you are holding in mind lack. In fact, right now, you may actually be completely OK financially. Take a look, be honest – are you OK right now? You exist, you are alive, most likely you have a place to live and sleep and food to eat.

But still, you are wanting more. You are not satisfied with what you have. That dissatisfaction is disapproval. So instead of judging that – be honest, acknowledge that you simply do not like your current financial situation. You want more!

Just notice if that brought up some disapproval or resistance. Maybe you feel greedy or ungrateful. There may be lots of feelings under this one. Money can be the most stuck area of all. You want money, but there is a feeling that it is not right to want money – it's not spiritual.

In my sessions the link between money and spirituality is strong, so it is very important to address this. I see that, through lifetimes, most people have made a vow of poverty. Perhaps they have been monks or nuns or just vowed never to be like that person who is rich because they are 'bad' people. Maybe even in this lifetime there has been the thought "I never want to be like …….. (a wealthy person) because they are not nice/good/honest …"

Of course, not all rich people are 'bad' people and you don't have to be poor to be spiritual, but it is hard to go against such a vow until you see it for what it is. Pull up all those feelings around money and wealthy people, and money and spirituality. Be honest about your beliefs, even if they make no sense. Write them down.

Then go back and look for the disapproval behind each of those thoughts. Welcome it up. You should be able to make a HUGE Broadway production out of all the material you can dig up here! Put it on stage, give all that judgment and disapproval some air time. Allow yourself to completely disapprove of rich people, or of money itself. Even be self-righteous about NOT being wealthy.

If you get stuck or uncomfortable it is just more resistance – it is just a feeling so welcome that up too. You can absolutely refuse to do this exercise if you like. Dig your heels in like Eeyore. Be a stubborn donkey. Judge, disapprove or whatever the feelings are. Just remember – they are JUST feelings. You can believe they are right and stop the process right now, or you can face the truth of yourself – see your thoughts and feelings for what they truly are – just feelings, fully acknowledge them, and see what happens. I invite you to find out, once and for all, if they really are sharks or if they were dolphins all along.

Each and every time you welcome up feelings of resistance and disapproval, whether it is about money, relationships, your body or anything else, they have less and less power. The areas of your life that cause you the most distress can be the very best for seeing this resistance. Once you start to see it and truly welcome it, have fun with it and accept it, you will see the REAL truth of yourself – that these are just feelings, they are not who you are.

Relationships/Love

If you are currently in the midst of a turbulent relationship or in love and pining for a love you cannot have – that may be good news! The more agonizing the situation seems to be, the more resistance is there. The more judgment and disapproval that is there the easier it is to see. It is actually the more subtle thoughts and feelings that are the hardest to spot, so for right now, the more 'pain' there seems to be, the better.

Just as with money, there may be two sides to the same coin. On the one hand you may love this person, and on the other you hate them. That leads to judgment of yourself for not being all loving and understanding. Then perhaps you think, like David did, that if only *they* would change everything would be alright. Or perhaps if YOU changed enough, twisted yourself to be 'perfect' for this other person then it would all be fine again. You go round and round and round in emotional circles, getting nowhere – all the while hating the situation, and wanting it to change, and desperately trying to suppress all those 'negative' emotions.

I have good news for you. I am giving you permission to be completely honest with yourself about how you feel. Notice, I said to be honest with YOURSELF. These are not feelings to share with anyone else – least of all the object of all these feelings. These feelings are within YOU. Just as it is none of your business what others think of you, neither is it any of their business what you think of them.

Think about it. You may already have tried telling them what you think of their behavior in the hopes they would see the light and change their ways. How did that work? How do you like it when someone tries to change you?

So instead of pushing away or trying to control all those pent up feelings – let 'em rip! The stage is all set up and ready to go, so put those feelings right up there in the spot light. Give them the space to strut, pout, rage, judge, be righteous, indignant, jealous, mad … bring it ALL up on stage and let it out. All those feelings ever wanted was to be acknowledged and let out of their cage.

If you still feel in emotional turmoil, check to see what you are resisting or disapproving of and bring that on stage too. If there is still emotional 'pain' there is judgment, so keep digging, keep giving those feelings their air time and *make it all bigger than life.*

If you are feeling 'I can't, it's all too painful' then bring that up on stage. Dig your heels in. 'I can't, I won't, I refuse' Make it the most stubborn, petulant little child you can possibly think of. When some of the initial energy goes out of it, start singing – 'I can't, I won't, I never, ever will …..'

Keep going until you see just how funny the whole thing is. THEN you are truly in acceptance. Now see how you feel. If it still isn't funny, that's OK, there is just more disapproval. That too is just a feeling that is waiting to be fully acknowledged then it, too, can join in the fun.

Now is a good time to take a quick look around your stage. Just see if there are any remaining feelings that are still sitting in a corner with their arms and legs crossed refusing to come out and play. Guilt may be lurking there. Guilt is one of the deeper feelings, because it can evoke so much judgment. Have a look for any remaining jealousy too.

Whatever you may find, remember, they are just feelings – no different to any others, except that you may have even more disapproval of them than the others. So first, invite the disapproval onto the stage. It may be the disapproval of whatever you thought you did, or did not do, that caused the guilt feeling. Or perhaps you now feel you should not be jealous. Any time there is a 'should not', it is disapproval – so have a 'shouldn't' party. Bring up all those 'shoulds' and 'shouldn'ts' onto the stage, give them a drink with an umbrella in it, turn up the music and party! Why not? They are there in your mind anyway, or they would not have shown up so might as well enjoy them!

As you become more and more accepting of yourself and your own feelings, start to notice how much more accepting, more at peace you are with that other person or with the situation. Does it seem as bad anymore?

Has anything on the outside changed? No. Nothing has changed at all, you have just chosen to be honest about your own feelings and accept them. That's it. You didn't try to change your feelings even – just acknowledge them.

Even though absolutely nothing has changed, you are probably already feeling like everything has changed – and you are right. As you look in the mirror, the reflection is no longer of judgment, anger, hurt, jealousy, or guilt. Now as you look at the reflection of you, you see stillness, peace, acceptance, maybe even love and joy. Whatever is inside of you is what will be reflected back to you – not only on the inside, but in time, in your outside world too.

Feelings are like layers of an onion, so if more come up – it is just another layer ready to be peeled away. The key is to be watchful for the disapproval and resistance. Once you have fully recognized it for what it is, then it can no longer bother you – and neither will your thoughts and feelings.

To really dig deep – make a list of your significant relationships throughout your life. Notice especially, any repeated patterns (eg. abuse, abandonment, betrayal, being misunderstood, mistrust etc). Now trace each pattern back to your very earliest memory – the first time you experienced it, and pull up all the judgment and disapproval you possibly can. The more thorough you can be with the first memory, the easier the rest will be. You may even find that by the time you get to the 3rd or 4th experience that they no longer have any energy on them.

As you 'clean up' on past relationships, you will start to become more at peace and loving within your own self. Then start to notice what happens in your outer world – with the check out person in the grocery store, other drivers, the people you work with and most particularly, your own family.

As you become more accepting and loving, the mirror that is your outer world will reflect that right back to you. You didn't change anything and you didn't try to change any*one* either, and yet everything has changed.

"I could feel the energy while you were working with (me). The feeling of peace and tranquility is still with me.............even after spending a day with my mother-in-law ....! Truly a relationship gain that was completely unexpected. Thank you" **Veronica Phelan**

Health and the Body

Here is another great source of judgment! The media has done a fabulous job in promoting the image of the 'perfect' body. The ones who have this 'perfect' shape and size – the models – spend hours a day exercising or doing make up or fussing over their food. Are they happy? Not so much, from what I hear. Who is it that says this is the best shape to have anyway? And who is it that believes this mystery voice?

Rubens was a very famous artist who is renowned for painting pictures of voluptuous women. Botticelli's cherubs were always chubby. In India it is a sign of wealth to be well rounded. Bottom line – what anyone else thinks of you is none of your business. Having got that out of the way, we are left with what YOU think of you. Do you love and accept your body or do you disapprove of it?

Before we go further into that, let's take a look at health. Once again there is an image of what a body 'should' be like and one of the criteria is it 'should' be healthy, fit, have energy etc. Of course, that is nice, but as with money and relationships as long as you are judging your body as not OK and wanting to change it, you are holding in mind lack and, effectively, dis-ease. When you are not at ease with your body in your mind and thinking, then you are holding in mind dis-ease.

A few years ago I 'tweeked' my back somehow and was in great pain. For a week I could barely move from my bed. At this time, I knew about the power of feelings and how important it is to love yourself etc. So I really worked at loving myself and my back, but the pain just wasn't shifting. Then I finally realized that I was loving my back, but I was NOT loving the pain! I didn't like the pain, so the pain stayed – because what you resist, persists. Well, when I saw this I did manage to send love to the pain, and it did eventually get better.

What I didn't know how to do then is to acknowledge the disapproval and resistance. Back then I was trying to override the disapproval with love. It did finally work, but it would certainly have been easier to FIRST truly acknowledge that I really hated the pain! It is much easier to be honest about such feelings than to try to change them. Of course, being honest and accepting the feelings changes them anyway!

So welcome up all those judgmental feelings. Think of all the things about your body that you do not like – whether it is sick in some way or if it is the shape you don't like. Have a disapproval party – the thoughts are there anyway, so be honest with yourself and acknowledge them. If it feels brutal to do this, that is resistance – so disapprove of disapproving. Notice all the 'I can'ts' and 'shouldn'ts'. As long as they are left unacknowledged, the judgments will be there about your body – so dig deep.

As you do this you may well start to 'hear' voices from the past – perhaps your parents' judgments about their own bodies that you have taken on. Just for a moment – become them, be your parent criticizing themselves, or you. They can be actors on your stage too.

This is just you and your own mind – no one else is listening. Notice any resistance or disapproval. By now you may be finding that as soon as you notice the disapproval, it vanishes. Just that little bit of total acknowledgment is enough for it to disappear. The faster it is disappearing, the more accepting you are of it. Conversely, if it still needs the full 5 minutes on stage, then there is still some resistance and disapproval of the disapproval. That's OK. Just put it up on stage – have some more fun with it!

You may even find, as I did, that you look forward to these times where you get to indulge in your feelings! I would enthusiastically anticipate a 'fun with feelings' session – only to find they had all disappeared! When you are in full acceptance of your feelings, they instantly become a non-issue and they are gone.

Now, to my mind, that is definite proof that it is the resistance and ONLY the resistance that keeps those feelings being an issue. So when you are completely OK with resistance, disapproval, judgment or whatever other form it shows up as, ALL feelings become a non-issue. Now you see yourself as the witness of those feelings, instead of identifying with them. They can come, they can go, but you are happy and at peace either way. Your happiness is no longer dependent on your feelings! Now that is Freedom!

Lester Levinson used to say that Freedom means it's OK to go left and it's OK to go right. In other words, it's OK to have pain or no pain, health or dis-ease, be fat or thin, short or tall, happy or sad, young or old. When you are in complete acceptance of all your feelings, you are no longer bothered – it is now OK to go left or to go right. That is Freedom – no more worries!

Work

By now you are probably getting the idea! If you are not happy with your work situation, then you want to change it. You are holding in mind that it is not OK. Since thought is creative, you will get more of what you are thinking – that your work situation is not OK! *Allow yourself to be honest* and see all the disapproval there. *Being honest and seeing the feelings is your ticket to Freedom.* If you notice you are judgmental of even having those disapproving feelings, then be honest about that too!

Once again, the only issue is the resistance to these thoughts and the disapproval of the thoughts and of your work. Take an honest look at your feelings. It could be that you have no work and you don't like that, or the work you have doesn't pay enough, you don't like the work you do, or you don't get on with your boss or co-workers. Here's a good one – you aren't happy in your work, but you think you should be because at least you have a job. Whenever there is a 'should', there is disapproval.

Take a moment to write it all down – just allow the thoughts to flow through onto the paper. Be completely honest – these are just thoughts; they cannot harm you or anyone else. You know the expression – 'Better out than in …' well it is most definitely true with feelings – let them out. What you do NOT need to do is share them with anyone else. These are entirely your own feelings. They actually have nothing to do with anyone else.

Now, if you are thinking how much you would really like to tell your boss or co-worker what you don't like about them – then do that. Do it in the privacy of your own mind, on your own personal stage. Make a whole production out of it. Set the scene and indulge. Tell them everything you feel. Just make sure you make it *bigger than life and very dramatic* so you become the witness.

That way, you get to see that these feelings are not really you – they are all just an act, a game. You will also find yourself in complete acceptance of those feelings, and suddenly they become a non-issue. Now look again at how you feel about your boss or co-worker – easier, lighter and more accepting?

Take a look at everything you wrote down. Take each thought and look for the disapproval, judgment or resistance. Set the scene on your stage and bring in the main characters – all those disapproving feelings! Let them out to play. Give them their 5 minutes of fame and glory on stage. Keep looking for the judgments until the original thought feels like a non-issue – it simply has no power. You know you are 'there' when it is OK with you if that thought stays around, or if it disappears. It is just a bunch of words with no meaning any more.

As you move on to each of the thoughts that you wrote down, you will most likely start to see that each of them has less and less energy behind it. As you allow yourself to be honest with the judgments and get to be completely Ok with it, you will start to see less and less judgment. You are effectively digging it all up by the roots, rather than trying to cut it down from the top. So take plenty of time on those first few thoughts, and you will probably find that the rest of that lengthy list is already a non-issue – just a bunch of words with no meaning.

Once again, you have changed absolutely nothing. You haven't even changed your feelings - just decided to accept them. And yet, as your inner world becomes more accepting and loving, just look at what is happening in your outer world!

If you are feeling angry and upset and you look in the mirror – what do you see? You see anger and upset. When you feel loving and joyful and look in the mirror – love and joy are reflected back to you. So it is in life.

If you drive down the road feeling angry, you *know* you will run into the one other person in the world who got out of bed on the wrong side and is also angry. The funny thing is, when you are in that happy, loving place – even if you DO run into that same person, it is no longer an issue. You can send them love and just drive on by to have a happy, loving day.

There was a time when I used to fight with my daughter almost daily. She would get mad and I would get mad right back at her. At first I tried taking HER to counseling! Of course, that didn't help much.

This situation was actually one of the main reasons that I started looking for answers for myself. As I worked on my feelings, I was able to deal with my own anger through accepting my feelings. Without changing anything, I found I was no longer angry. I simply didn't have the buttons any more for her to push. Then she, too, stopped being so angry.

I had gotten her some foam balls to squeeze when she felt really angry. One day, we were cleaning out her room and we came across them and found one of them had holes in it.

She said "We need to get another one" to which I replied, "When is the last time you were angry and needed to use them?"

It was at that moment that I truly saw what an incredible impact this work has had on my life. If nothing else had ever changed – that, by itself, was worth every second of the work I have put in.

Spirituality

If you find you are getting stuck with doing any part of this process of looking fully at the disapproval, then check in to see if you have the belief that 'it's not spiritual to be negative'. I know that many courses and trainings I have done in the past have focused on the positive aspects and tended to veer away from the 'negative'. All this really does is to put a thin layer of oil over those feelings – but they are still there.

When we try to focus on the positive and have loving thoughts, it actually sets up more resistance to the not-quite-so-loving thoughts. By focusing on those less-than-loving thoughts, we are actually loving them and allowing them to dissolve. What you resist persists. So however much love you pour into your thinking and your life, it is still important to address the non-loving feelings. In fact, when you do let them out, you will find so much more love, joy, gratitude and peace – it will just bubble up quite naturally without having to 'try' to be loving and positive.

So take a look and see if you are just generally disapproving of 'negative' thoughts and feelings. I don't tend to consider thoughts to be either positive or negative. They aren't really good or bad – they just 'are'. Of course, if you don't like the word 'negative' then that is just another actor to put up on your stage and play with! Just another feeling!

If you find yourself wanting to push this away and not look at those negative feelings, then there is resistance. Before you start judging THAT, remember – these are all just feelings.

This is the place I got pretty stuck for a while and where I created my hall of mirrors. I had been to many self-improvement trainings, done self-esteem courses and most of it seemed to me to be about focusing on the positive and being all loving. Even then it felt unreal to me, although I tried - pretending to love people when, frankly, I didn't! Now I can see that, of course, I found it hard to love others because I had so many judgments about myself!

Now that may well have been my interpretation of those courses, because I simply did not like looking at those other thoughts and feelings. Primarily, it was VERY uncomfortable to look at the judgments I had of myself because I truly felt like a 'bad' person.

I was devastated if anyone thought badly of me. I wanted to crawl away and hide under a rock. Then I would keep thinking about whatever they had said and digging an even deeper hole of disapproval for myself.

The hardest one to accept and the last one to 'go' was when I felt unjustly 'accused' of something. It felt like the end of the world, and my mind would be extremely busy trying to work out how to prove that they were wrong and that I was really an OK person! I am almost surprised I never became a trial lawyer or something, so I could stand up for the wrongly accused! Of course, I was too busy trying to fight my own battles to worry about everyone else's!

If you can relate to any of this, then I am so glad you have this book! I really hope that I can save you from all the suffering I put myself through in the name of righteousness!

I watched a movie recently where one of the characters told his son, "You only have to be brave for 20 seconds". So I encourage you to be brave for just 20 seconds, pull up all those scary and painful feelings, and put them up on stage.

If you can put yourself into this 100%, then in 20 seconds you can change your life – not just a little bit but completely. In just 20 seconds of over-dramatized feelings up on your stage, you will see them for what they truly are – JUST feelings. What you thought of as sharks, you will now see as dolphins.

Persist – keep going with any and all of those 'sharks' and soon enough there will be no more sharks – only dolphins swimming around your internal world.

Then, what is so amazing is that your external world will start to reflect back this shift on the inside. When your inside world is full of judgment and disapproval, that is what will show up on the outside too. You will see lots of things to be judgmental about, and you will see others judging everything too.

When you shift your internal perspective from sharks to dolphins, your outer world will also be filled with dolphins. So if, as a spiritual being, your heart's desire is to live in a world of love, joy, gratitude, peace and harmony, then the permanent way to get there is by actually focusing 100% on everything that is NOT that. Try being loving, joyful and grateful for your own feelings! I invite you to try it. Instead of trying hard to float above the mud and the sharks, be brave for just 20 seconds, invite them up on your stage, and see that they are really dolphins.

Once you have proved to yourself that all those disapproving thoughts are just feelings, they are just dolphins and not sharks, then you are Free. No longer will you be run by fear or judgment of those feelings. You can jump off the surf board any time you like and swim with them – they no longer bother you.

So now take another look at the belief 'It's not spiritual to be negative'. How does it feel now? Is it still true? Is there really such a thing as 'negative' or even 'positive' anymore? Do you still disapprove of 'negative' feelings? Or have you been brave for 20 seconds and now know, beyond a shadow of doubt, that they are all just feelings – and dolphins, nothing to fear or judge.

If you aren't quite there yet, that's OK. You have been trained well, and the habit of disapproval has been there for a long, long time. Just keep at it. Be brave for 20 seconds and see, at the end of it, if you feel even just a little bit lighter. Even just reading this book may give you a sense of what is possible. Finally you know that you don't have to disapprove of ANY of your thoughts or feelings. Knowing that alone can change your world.

Still think you can change things with disapproval?

Sometimes people are afraid that if they accept what is, then it will never change. Actually, it is the opposite. If you do NOT first accept what is, then it will never change. As long as you want it to change, you are holding in mind that it has not changed and it is stuck.

Let me clarify this a little. When I talk about accepting what is, I am not talking about a place of apathy and giving up. That is Eeyore's world (from Winnie the Pooh) where nothing goes right and he is always a, very, very sad donkey. Eeyore might say "There's no point trying, nothing ever works out anyway." If that is what you are still feeling, that's fine. That too is a feeling. Putting those Eeyore feelings up on stage is my favorite. Be Eeyore, be apathy, be depression – just make it bigger than life!

The acceptance I am talking about is a very high energy – it is right up there with love, joy and gratitude. There is no pushing away of negative feelings, the feelings simply aren't there. In fact, as you get into this place of true acceptance, love and peace, you may notice that it really isn't a feeling at all. Feelings tend to come and go, but this is a place of Being – you have started to uncover your True Self, the Being that you are and always have been – it was just covered up with all the feelings. We will come back to this in the final chapter.

So, what if it is actually true that by accepting it, it will not change? There you are in acceptance and nothing has changed. Ask yourself, would you rather be in this situation (money, relationships, health) not liking it, resisting it and unhappy - or would you prefer to be in acceptance, OK with what is?

Since I know all my readers are very smart, I expect that you decided it is more preferable to be at peace with what is. Just notice here if you are still attached to your outer world changing. If you are trying to do this process to accept your feelings so that your outer world will change, then there is still some disapproval of yourself and of your world.

The key is to come to complete acceptance of yourself and your world. The way to get there is to accept your feelings exactly the way they are. And the way to get to that point is to acknowledge all the disapproval, judgment and resistance. When you truly are OK with the judgment and disapproval, then that hall of mirrors becomes like a domino effect. As the deepest judgment is accepted, the first domino falls, and all the other dominos follow suit. As you accept those resistant feelings, the mirrors start to disappear until there is only one left. There is only one image, and what it reflects back to you is acceptance, love, peace, joy and harmony. Not so bad!

So what is there to lose? Even if nothing else changed – you just find yourself in a place of acceptance and peace, how bad is that?

How I found my new home through acceptance

There came a time in my 'process' when I knew it was time to move. At that time, I was living near Sedona, Arizona and I got the message that I would be moving – not just to another house, but to another state. I had been living in Arizona ever since I moved from England to the States 20 years earlier, so this was no small thing. Plus, my children were in middle school and high school – not necessarily a great time to move.

The first confirmation that this move was meant to be came when I first talked to the children about it. Without any hesitation they both said 'Yes' to the move, and the sooner the better. A month later we were on the road – a 2 day drive up to Oregon, having sold or given away over 50% of our belongings. We kept what was essential and what was of value to us.

Some of the last things to go were the couches. I loved those couches – they reclined and were so comfortable. I had almost decided to just keep them when we had a call from a prospective buyer. I muted the phone and asked my kids – "Do we really want to sell the couches or shall we keep them?" Without hesitation my son said "Sell them. It will work out". Reluctantly, I agreed.

When we left Arizona, we had no idea where we would be living. The move was so fast that I had not had time to go up and find a place. A friend of mine had moved up to Bend, Oregon a few years previously and, as we were driving up, she offered us a place to stay in her boyfriend's cabin a few miles out of town. They now lived in town so it was fully furnished, but empty – perfect for the 3 of us until we could find a home. I will always be most grateful for that time, as it allowed me time to 'arrive', get a feel of Bend and, ultimately, find the neighborhood we were destined to live. It also gave me the time to learn a huge lesson in acceptance and surrendering to Divine Guidance!

The first area that I thought would be perfect for us just did not seem to be coming together. Finally, I realized I wasn't looking in the right area. Although we had a lovely place to stay, we were all anxious to have our own home so to feel back at square one caused some work in acceptance! What happened, though, was that out of that peace of acceptance, it became clear that I should look in the north part of town.

The first day I drove up north there was a road block and detour, which took me through a neighborhood that caused my jaw to drop. THIS was what I was looking for! It was a neighborhood of homes on 2 or more acres, and all irrigated so every home had lush looking lawns and deciduous trees. Bend is high desert, so unless there is irrigation it is dry. I did not miss the English weather, but every time I visited my family in England I realized how much I loved the green. Even though it felt very rural, it was actually only a few minutes from some of my favorite stores. My son's one request was to be somewhere rural but still close to everything. Clearly this was 'our' neighborhood.

Then another issue arose – no houses for rent in this area. As I continued to keep welcoming up all of my judgment (I can't do this, how am I supposed to find a place here, this will never work ...) and accepting it all, it became easier and easier to just allow things to fall into place.

When you do this process of accepting all feelings, your mind will go quiet. That is when the intuition or Divine Guidance can be heard. It is always there, we just don't hear it when the mind is busy. So the very next day, as I was in the place of allowing, I received a clear message to call the one spiritual contact I had in the Bend area. We had never met – just exchanged emails briefly before I left Arizona. Turned out, he lived in this very neighborhood. He had weekly Oneness deeksha (blessing exchange) groups at his house, and his daughter was just a year older than mine.

Over the next two weeks as I continued to 'allow' – everything fell into place. I went to the next deeksha meeting, felt immediately welcomed, sat next to a woman from the same neighborhood who put me in contact with a realtor ..... and I found a house, right in this neighborhood – just 2 houses away from my new friend and the deeksha meetings. Not only did we get it for under market rent, the lawn service was 'thrown in' and there was still some furniture in the house that they were willing to lend us – including some great couches! In fact, everything we had sold and needed was in the house.

I have never been very adept at making decisions. I used to agonize over 'important' decisions for days. In the past, this would most definitely have been one of those times. Was this the right house, what about the schools, was Bend even the right place for us … etc. By the time we saw the house for the first time, however, it was extremely clear to me that accepting all the mind chatter and surrendering to Divine Guidance was definitely the easier way. I also asked for complete clarity. If this was the right house for us, please bring it to us. If it was not, please just let it disappear.

We had seen one house earlier and I had used this process. I accepted all the feelings about it (was it right, what if there wasn't another house, perhaps we should ….), surrendered it to the Divine, and asked for clarity. In that instance the house just 'disappeared'. Even though I filled in an application to rent it, we never heard another word about it – clearly not our home.

This second house was the absolute opposite – it was yes all the way – even down to the furniture they left behind! The only decision I really made was accepting all the feelings, allowing my mind to become quiet and asking for crystal clear guidance. So much easier than the mind struggle method I used to use!

PEACE

How changing nothing allows everything to change

You are the center of your life.

Life may sometimes seem like a tornado or hurricane. All around you things are going on that can so easily suck you in. Just turn on the news and watch stories of floods, fires, murders, starving children. Then there are political races and 'experts' on every imaginable subject arguing about who is right. There is a constant barrage of issues 'out there' in the world.

Closer to home, it is the same but on a different scale. Your children may be leaving home and going 'out there' into that storm of world events. You argue with your family members about your different political views, ways to raise the kids, which bills to pay first, whether you should eat this or that, or who left the top off the toothpaste. Any one of these can be a friendly conversation, or an all-out fight.

Bring it even closer to home and see the arguments you have with yourself. How am I going to get enough money to pay the bills and survive? What should I wear to meet my friends? I want to lose weight, but that means exercise and eating less. My life is passing me by. If only I could change, or they would change, I could be happy.

Each of these is just another circle of the tornado swirling around you. The further 'out there' you go, the more out of control it may feel. After all, what can you really do about world events? You try hard to do something about your family affairs and, even closer to home, you know you <u>can</u> change how you eat or exercise.

The eye of the storm is always perfectly still. You are the center of your life. The further 'out there' you go to try to change it, the more you can get caught up in the storm. If xyz political party won the election everything would be OK. If my spouse or children did ABC … I could be happy. If I meditated more, exercised, ate better …. Blah, blah, blah.

Right in the center is stillness and peace. When you let go of trying to change yourself, your family, the world, and come into your center, there you will always find peace. It is the peace that is completely independent of what is going on around you. It is not an emotion; it is You, the True You.

The way into that place of stillness is by doing nothing – just Being instead of trying to change your feelings and emotions. Let them swirl around you. You do not have to swirl with them. By acknowledging them and accepting them, you are moving into that place of Inner Peace and stillness. You aren't trying to change the emotions, just stepping back, out of the path of the storm, into your True Self.

Now perhaps you are starting to see that You are not your feelings. At the beginning, you identified with your feelings. I AM angry, I AM sad, I AM afraid. As you come to accept your feelings for what they truly are – JUST feelings that cannot hurt you – you can start to identify with the True You.

Floating down the stream

Remember when you decided to let go of trying to paddle upstream, fighting your feelings and emotions tooth and nail to get back to a familiar place? Now you have gotten smart and let go of the struggle, accepted your feelings for what they are and are happily floating downstream, with the current. As you turn around, you see you are floating into a far more beautiful and wonderful place. This is your center, your place of Peace. Now as you merrily float downstream, you find you are the witness. You see on either side of the river, the places where, before, you might have gotten out and tried to change things. You know – the world, your family, yourself. Remember that 'old' life?

Now, from your center of Peace you can watch the world go by, see all the family dynamics, and witness your own thoughts and feelings. At any time you want, you can stretch out your hand or step out of your center and BE in that crazy world again. It is always there, just as your center of stillness and Peace has always been there, right where You are.

At any time you choose, you can BE in this place of Peace and still be in the world. You can move around the world, be in the world, be a part of your family, live your life – all the time being in this place of stillness and Peace, witnessing the 'other' as it passes you by.

What does your ego have to say?

Just as You are not your feelings or emotions, You are also not your mind/ego. Your thoughts, feelings and emotions are a function of your mind/ego, which is its job. The mind/ego is like a computer, you program it and it feeds back to you what you have programmed in.

So as a child, perhaps your mother was afraid for you. She saw you walking into the street and ran after you, with fearful thoughts of you being hit by a car. She saved you, so you program into your computer that in order to be safe you first need fear.

Then your father gets mad at you for leaving your toys on the floor where he just tripped over them. He makes you pick them up and then he is happy. So you program in that to get what you want you must get angry.

You have already decided that to get love, you should do what your mother or father wants you to do – that is a major part of your programming. So when you 'fall' in love your ego/mind programming tells you to twist yourself around and do what your 'love' wants, and they will always love you. Then after a while, you aren't happy. They may still love you, but you still aren't happy. You are 'out there' swirling around in this storm of life and the further you move away from You, your center, the more out of control your life feels.

Your ego/mind will tell you that in order to be happy, you must 'get out there' and change the world around you. It will tell you that you must feel fear and anger to get what you want. There is nothing bad about your ego/mind, it is simply doing its job – just like any computer program.

You grew up believing that you ARE your ego/mind. That is just what life taught us. It is what the majority of the world believed, so you did too. There is nothing wrong in that at all. It is just the way it always was. However, you were also smart enough to see that this wasn't working out so well. You followed the ego/mind programming and life was NOT a bunch of roses.

What did you learn as a child about feelings?

In a recent teleconference call, I asked the participants what they learned about feelings as a child.

Here are some of their responses:-

"I was too sensitive, keep quiet..... Expressing feeling or speaking about it was unsafe and dangerous to my life.... Others have greater problems than you so suck it up! ....Not manly to be too emotional.... Your feelings don't count.... Stop daydreaming & stop being so theatrical.... Stop being dramatic....keep it to yourself... Your feelings are selfish... I got the feeling I was too intense so I hide my emotions.... Stop crying or I'll give you something to cry about... As a child I was too much"

So you can clearly see where these people learned that their feelings were not OK, and I'm sure you can also relate from your own childhood. They learned to disapprove of themselves and to hide their feelings. As children, they did this so their parents would love them. Their parents were most likely uncomfortable with their own feelings, so of course they taught their children the same thing.

These are decisions made with an undiscriminating mind as children. It was self-preservation. If you did what your parents wanted, then they would continue to love you, feed you and take care of you. So if they didn't want you to show emotion, then you stuffed them down.

As adults, you can see that these decisions no longer serve you. Now, with a discriminating mind, it makes more sense to just be OK with all your feelings. It served you as a child to hide your emotions, and now it serves you far better to accept your feelings and ego/mind just the way it is.

Some false beliefs about Ego

1. **The ego is bad**: The ego is really just like a computer. It does what it is programmed to do – nothing more and nothing less. It still has a valuable function in taking care of things – reminding you to brush your teeth, eat, pick up the kids from school. What you are de-programming is the part that says "You have to brush your teeth or else …. All your teeth will fall out" That programming – usually learned as children, really does not help any more. In accepting that it exists and seeing, with a discriminating mind, that it no longer serves you, you can let it go. So the ego really isn't bad, or good, it just exists as a part of You.

2. **The ego will fight back if you try to change things**: I have heard that when you try to let things go from the ego that the ego will fight back. The way I see it is that as you let go of the thoughts and feelings, what is left is resistance and disapproval – which may feel as if the ego is 'fighting back'. Those feelings just want to be acknowledged

too! If, as I have suggested, you START with the disapproval and resistance, you are acknowledging the roots and the rest of the thoughts and feelings are a non-issue.

3. **The ego must be destroyed**!: Remember that thought is creative – if you think that the ego is bad, evil, the enemy – then it is! It will feel as if you must fight it to the death. As you know, I like easy! In my reality my ego is neither good, nor bad. It most definitely does not need to be destroyed. What you push against will push back. If you love and accept it just as it is, there need be no fighting and you will see that You are not your ego – just as You are not your computer. You can shout at your computer, even smash it, but it still won't change those programs you created. In acknowledging the issue and showing it some love and respect, most likely the answer will just show up.

Challenges reap rewards

The good thing about life's challenges is that it is most often out of the biggest challenges that you reap the greatest rewards. It is the time when you feel like you have been thrown in at the deep end without a life jacket that you start to learn to swim. Those are the moments that you looked deeper within yourself for the answers.

As you find the way to accepting your feelings and being the witness of them, you may actually start to welcome the challenges. Instead of a feeling of "oh no, not more stuff" it becomes "Ahh, another lesson that will get me even deeper into my center of Peace."

Quick note: If you do find yourself thinking, "Oh no, not more stuff" – remember, this is just resistance and disapproval, just another feeling. Welcome it up on stage and give it its 5 minutes of glory. If you have not yet fully experienced doing this, then you may be thinking that your 'stuff' will take way longer than 5 minutes. Well, you may be surprised.

Just as with little Suzie, who so desperately wants her parents attention – when she does get their full, undivided attention it takes just a moment before she is quite happy again and off she goes to play. So, too, with your feelings. All it takes is to fully face them, and almost instantly they have no more power.

It is like a phone telling you that you have a message. It will keep beeping or blinking the light at you until you give it attention. You don't even have to read the text or listen to the message. The phone is programmed to know when you have noticed the message and the beeping noise, the flashing light stops immediately.

What does not work is if you just look at the phone and say "OK I see that there is a message but I don't want to be bothered with it right now so stop beeping at me". Neither does it work to say to yourself, "I know I have all these feelings but I just can't be dealing with them right now so just go away". Our ego/mind program is actually set to beep <u>even louder</u> when we ignore it!

It really does take far less time to take a full on look at those feelings than to try to ignore them or change them. You have already tried ignoring them or pushing them away. That didn't work, so time for something different. If you have not already tried this out for yourself, then I suggest you take another look at the chapter on resistance. Give it a shot. You have nothing to lose (except painful feelings) and everything to gain – finding your center of Peace.

Inner Peace

Inner Peace is not a feeling, it is not a function of the ego at all, it is your True Self – your Real Nature. When you find that place within you – that has always been there, you will see how natural it feels. It is a sense of 'Of course, this is who I am'. It really is no big deal! It is here that you start to tap into your unlimited potential.

1. **Intuition/Divine Guidance:** In this place of peace your mind becomes still and quiet. There are still thoughts, but it is easy to be still any time you choose. In this place of quiet you can hear messages from your higher self – your intuition. Ask and you

shall receive. Ask for clarity, direction, guidance and then be still and listen. When the mind is quiet you can hear the answers. Tapping into Universal consciousness in this way is like tapping into Omniscience – the place of all knowing. Everyone has access to it – still your mind, and you will have unlimited access too.

2. **Better Relationships:** As you let go of trying so hard to change yourself and your own feelings, you will also find you no longer feel the need to change others either. In your place of peace they will no longer bother you. If they do – it's just a little more resistance and disapproval. As your inner self of love and peace shows up more and more, so too will your outer world reflect back greater love and peace. Be aware that as your vibration rises, as it will, some people around you will rise in their vibration to match yours. Others may not be willing or ready for that, and some friendships may fall away. It is all perfect – for them and for you. Just allow the harmony to unfold.

3. **Ask and you shall receive:** As your own vibration rises, you will be closer to the vibration of manifestation. Take care of what you hold in mind as you may well receive it! I once had the thought that I really only needed half a loaf of bread out on the counter. A short while later my dogs obliged by pulling it down off the counter and eating half of the loaf! I recommend that whatever you ask for –

whether for yourself or for others – that you always ask for whatever is the highest and best for you, or them. I have asked for some things in the past that have not shown up. Later, I realized that they simply were not in my best interest at that time.

EASY

Thank You for travelling this journey with me.

I hope you have found it helpful in your life and your
world and I wish you love, joy and peace.

I would like to leave you with just two thoughts:-

'This can be easy'

'You are closer than you think'

Appendix

Lester Levinson has been one of my teachers along this path of self-discovery. In his own process he came to a good place where he felt happy and at peace. He could have stopped there, but he didn't. His view was that if this was how it felt to have one piece of the cake, how would it be to have the whole cake? He found his whole cake and has been an inspiration to me and many, many others to never, ever stop – until you have your whole cake.

Lester was the instigator of the method of Releasing, which is what I used extensively and took me from depressed to happy. There are several organizations that teach this technique including *The Release Technique* and *The Sedona Method*.

Florence Scovel Shinn: One book has been extremely influential in my life since a friend gave it to me when I was in my 20's. It is called, appropriately, **"The Game of Life and How to Play It"** and was written by Florence Scovel Shinn. In it she talks about the Divine Plan of our lives.

She describes this as the four square of perfect Health, Wealth, Love and perfect self-expression.

The Oneness University: I did the Oneness training with **Rev Kerry Chinn**. It had a very profound effect on my spiritual awakening process. There are many trainers and deeksha givers (Oneness blessings givers) around the world.

All of these people and organizations came to me through guidance – whether I was aware of the guidance or not! Ask for your own guidance as to what is right for you.

Earlier in the book, I touched on the importance of our intentions. My intention has been to have my Divine Plan – my very best life, the whole cake. You can have your cake – and eat it too! Be grateful for each slice of cake as it comes to you and keep your sights set on having the whole cake. There is nothing you have to do or be differently 'out there' in the world. It is all within you right now. That place of stillness, happiness and Peace is right in the center of You, just as You are in the center of your life. ALL the answers are within You.

It is from that place within you that you will start to really change your life. A ballerina doing a pirouette starts by slowly spinning. Then, as she pulls her limbs in tight to her side, she goes faster and faster. It is quite extraordinary to watch. It is as if there is this moment of stillness as she comes out of it and it seems to me as if, in that moment, the world around her has changed.

As you start to experience this place of Peace within you it is almost as if the world around you pauses for a second. In that moment there are no issues, no stress, only stillness and harmony. Nothing has changed on the 'outside', you have found this place within in you. What HAS changed is how you see the world. In that moment it is a peaceful, harmonious world.

The more you view the world as peaceful and harmonious, the more YOUR world will be exactly that. Without needing to do anything to change the outer world, it starts to change anyway. It is in that still, quiet place that you can start to hear your own guidance, intuition, or whatever you like to call it. Listen and trust. This is You, the real You. You have always been there, right there, where You are.

Welcome Home.

For current links to the above organizations please go to:-

www.ArchAngelAlignments.com/Links

AUTHOR

Jenny La Fontaine was born in England and moved to Arizona, USA in 1991. She now lives in Bend, Oregon with her two children.

Jenny is an Intuitive Messenger. She works with the Archangels giving Intuitive Guidance for all kinds of life issues, as well as doing Clearings and Alignments. Jenny is guided to see programs, beliefs and other blocks in this life time and past life times and ask for them to be cleared to help her clients connect with their True Self. She works from the premise 'ask and you shall receive, and so it is.' She calls it the easy button.

Jenny's mission is to help raise the consciousness of the planet, one person at a time. This book is designed to help everyone who has a true desire to connect with who they really are. Jenny shows how this is not only possible but easy - through acceptance.

Jenny's own personal transformation really started after her father died in 2007. A year later her 20 year marriage endedand she was a single mother with 2 school age children. In 2009 she came across 'The Release Technique'.

Jenny spent2 1/2 years fully immersed in releasing and went from depressed to being happy most of the time. It was then that she started to learn the power of confronting and accepting negative feelings rather than trying to push them away or pretend they did not exist.

One of her teachers said "If the mind is creative then we can make this easy". Shortly after that Jenny started doing clearings, working with the Archangels and became an Intuitive Messenger. Even though she had never considered doing this kind of work before, she says it is completely natural to her as if she has always been doing it.

Jenny says "It was when I came to a place of complete acceptance of myself and my feelings that I could clearly receive Intuitive Guidance. It was from that point that I followed Divine Guidance more than my ego/mind guidance! Life definitely became easier and started to flow. Now I am rarely bothered by anything and I live in an almost constant place of joy"

FREE Audio

'Fun with Feelings' Guided Meditation

With

Jenny La Fontaine

Jenny leads you through the Fun with Feelings Guided Meditation. This simple and fun exercise could change your life! Jenny brings fun and play to those feelings that up to now may have felt overwhelming and a never-ending emotional spin cycle.

- Step by step guide to putting your feelings 'on stage'
- Transform your 'negative' feelings into FUN
- Learn how to deal with ANY uncomfortable feelings – easily, anytime
- See the root cause of ANY 'negative' feeling and know exactly how to free yourself from these lower energies.
- Change from being immersed in feelings to being the witness and have fun watching them!
- This simple exercise can free you forever from getting caught in the emotional spin cycle.

"What a great exercise/tool you gave us with the total acceptance of EVERY feeling, no matter what it looks like. Not only will this make life easier but it will also help me to accept myself in all the totality that I am. I am not just this or that, I am ALL of it. Thank you so much! "Katharina Roth

Get Your FREE instant download of

'The Fun with Feelings' Meditation Audio Here:-

www.ChangeEverythingBook.com/Audio

To learn more and to contact the author go to:-

www.ArchAngelAlignments.com

www.ChangeEverythingBook.com

Jenny La Fontaine

Made in the USA
San Bernardino, CA
16 June 2015